Slightly Foxed Editions

MR TIBBITS'S CATHOLIC SCHOOL

SLIGHTLY FOXED EDITIONS

No. 15

MR TIBBITS'S
CATHOLIC SCHOOL

Ysenda Maxtone Graham

Illustrations by Kath Walker

First published by Slightly Foxed in 2011
in a limited edition of 2,000 copies
of which this is copy No.

704

Slightly Foxed Ltd
67 Dickinson Court
15 Brewhouse Yard
London ECIV 4JX

A CIP catalogue record for this book is available from the British Library.

ISBN 978-1-906562-27-4

Printed by Smith Settle, Yeadon, West Yorkshire

Contents

Preface

There are two sorts of school stories. Much the most popular, of course, are those that observe the drama of school life through the prism of the pupils' imagination. Malory Towers, the Chalet School adventures, Jennings and Darbishire, Harry Potter, Billy Bunter all belong to this addictive genre. My father, who was born in 1902, used to say that the essential thing to realize about such books is that they are really about class; that in his boyhood, it was not the privately educated who were devotees of Frank Richards's chronicles of Greyfriars, but those who attended 'government schools' and liked imagining themselves wearing an Eton collar and being given six of the best in the Cloisters.

I am not entirely convinced by this analysis, but I shall return to it. Meanwhile, it is worth noting that there is another type of school story, no less gripping, especially to those of us who have ourselves entered, however briefly, into the strange world of teaching, especially teaching in a private school. These are the stories in which the principal characters are not the children, but the teachers themselves. I am thinking of such masterpieces as Ivy Compton-Burnett's *Pastors and Masters*, or *More Women than Men*; Evelyn Waugh's *Decline and Fall* or, what is in some ways the best of such books, G. F. Bradby's *The Lanchester Tradition*, a classic comedy about the liberalizing headmaster of Rugby and the torment he caused to his conservative-minded staff.

One of the things brought out by such masterpieces is that almost all those who become schoolteachers, especially in a school for 7- to 13-year-olds, have elected to be seen through the eyes of those who may well idolize or hate them, but will also (especially in England) refuse to take them entirely seriously. They have therefore sacrificed not merely their lives but their dignity – in the words of the scornful father of one of Ivy Compton-Burnett's characters, they have chosen to 'humiliate themselves for a pittance'. And yet, two other ingredients need to be mentioned. There is the essential seriousness of their task – teachers of this age group are helping to form and fill human minds. They have far more influence than university professors. There is a truth, which this book makes inescapable, in the old adage that if you have a child at 7 you have it for life. There is another, also wonderfully illustrated here: that prep schools are places of hilarity. John Betjeman, later Poet Laureate, and a man who was full of laughter, always used to say that he had never laughed so much as during the year in which he was the cricket master at a small private school near Gerrards Cross.

It is an assemblage of such facts and notions that gives extraordinary pathos and humour to the obese figure of the founder-headmaster of St Philip Neri's school, Kensington, as depicted in Ysenda Maxtone Graham's *Mr Tibbits's Catholic School*. Ysenda Maxtone Graham is an entirely original, imaginative intelligence. As an ardent member of her fan-club, I am perpetually amazed that she is not as famous as Stevie Smith, Jane Austen or Dorothy Parker, for she is one of the great humorists, with an entirely distinctive 'take' on the world. Her previous books – *The Church Hesitant*, a study of the Church of England, and *The Real Mrs Miniver*, the story of her grandmother, the author Jan Struther – are works of non-fiction, but when I think of them both it is as if I am remembering much-loved novels. This is because Ysenda has the passionate nosiness of the novelist. It is also because she knows how a tiny detail can bring a whole character, a whole scene, to life.

The subject of her new book is a small Roman Catholic private school, started in Kensington in 1934 by a man called Richard Tibbits. At first, when I heard this, I assumed that she had made up the surname, but of course, the gods or the muses knew whom they wanted as the author of the book. Without knowing it, Mr Tibbits had been in Maxtone Graham-land all his life, but he waited, like Michelangelo's slaves imprisoned in marble, until she arrived posthumously with her chisel to make him immortal.

This unusual school history has all the charm and excitement of an Ealing Comedy. One of the details that will stay with me forever is Mr Tibbits's luncheon routines. He had a glass of sherry beforehand and drank red wine 'with his cheese', while the boys were munching their way through their spam with mash, tinned spaghetti and other horrors. (Finishing what was on one's plate was compulsory and if a boy was unable to finish, the entire school was required to wait in the dining-room until he did so.)

This, together with Mr Tibbits's fearful temper, and his habit of hitting the boys with a slipper (some remembered with a hard shoe) if they did badly in their Latin tests, would imply that St Philip's was a cruel place. This is not the impression any fair-minded reader will derive from Ysenda Maxtone Graham's account. In his extraordinary way, Mr Tibbits obviously loved children and was a good teacher. (Another detail I shall always remember is his taking them to swim in the Chelsea baths. He was extremely fat and by this stage wheezy. If any child in the pool got into difficulties, Mr Tibbits, fully clothed, naturally, would hold out a walking stick over the chlorinated waters for their hands to grasp.)

The school was begun in strange circumstances. Mr Tibbits was a member of the Church of England who converted to Catholicism. At the Brompton Oratory one day, a priest remarked that there were no good private schools for Catholic boys in that region of London and Tibbits offered to found one. He bought a house – 6 Wetherby Place, just off the Gloucester Road – and in the early days he did not merely teach the children, he also did the school run, fetching them from their front doors and delivering them back in the afternoons in his rackety old car. Later, as the school grew in numbers, Mr Tibbits married a fellow chain-smoker. It was she who was responsible for choosing the disgusting menus, and she remained, like her brother-in-law and her nephew, who later joined the staff and became headmaster, C of E. It was for this reason that the school began a near quarter of a century's separation from the Oratory.

There was a strong class element in all this. Class has
been an all but unmentionable subject since Nancy
Mitford made herself so unpopular by pointing out
that the use of such words as 'looking-glass' or 'loo' or
'chimney-piece' could be taken as social indicators.
Yet, as Ysenda Maxtone Graham is bold enough to see,
you cannot really write a social history of Roman
Catholicism in England without grasping the nettle.
She does so mercilessly and hilariously. The dilemma
facing many middle- to upper-middle-class converts to
Roman Catholicism in the middle years of the twentieth century was that they were joining a church
which was chiefly composed of the class known as 'lace
curtains Irish'. These converts, who were usually accus-
tomed to High Church rituals, tended to go to church
at the Brompton Oratory, which was founded by and
for converts. The educational 'problem' outlined by the
Oratory Father to Mr Tibbits was not, of course, that
there were no good Catholic schools in London, but
that there were no such schools for people like the congregation of the Oratory. The years of estrangement
from the Oratory are described with especial frankness.
An Irish Carmelite became the school chaplain, and he
had to put up with such questions from Mrs Tibbits,
when a beggar appeared at the kitchen door, as, 'Is he
Irish?'

Many readers of the book – including myself – will feel rather like the little proletarians described by my father who bought the boy's story paper the *Magnet* not because they themselves attended schools with cloisters and Latin mottoes, but because they wanted to see how the other half lived. In this case, it is to see not how a half, but how a tiny minority within a minority have lived – the little splinter group of middle- to upper-class Catholic children who needed to be taken to Mass and prepared for First Communion without the faint embarrassment of doing so in the company of those from very differing home backgrounds.

Ysenda Maxtone Graham's beady eye sees how revealing are the surnames of the old boys.

> The surname 'Galli' prompts us to ask: how international was the 1950s clientele? Were the surnames of St Philip's boys (as they are now) a seductive mixture of exotic European and English recusant, with the occasional modest square English surname thrown in (converts, Anglicans, etc)? It seems as if the answer is yes . . .

Even today, especially among Roman Catholics, the question of class within the English Catholic community causes anguish. This book shows that such anguish is misplaced. Class is an essentially comic thing. And it is only one of the ingredients in this book. What the author has done is to see the school as something like one of the One Hundred Objects through which the Director of the British Museum has chosen to tell the history of the world. By concentrating on this eccentric household in Kensington, with its often anguished staff, and its often amused pupils, she gives us an extraordinary microcosm of what has been happening offstage in the last seventy years, both in the Church and in the world.

Perhaps one of the book's strengths is its author's very slight distance from her subject. She is the mother of boys who have attended St Philip's, and she is also intensely musical. Her descriptions of the liturgy in the Little Oratory and of the value for young people of learning liturgical music are especially telling. At the book's heart, after all, is the essentially rather serious fact that nearly all the parents who have chosen St Philip's for their sons have done so because of a set of profoundly held religious beliefs. Ysenda Maxtone Graham, as a member of the C of E (the 'Church Hesitant'), is able to feel the 'Eucharistic elation' of the school Masses. But she also writes movingly of the science master who lost his faith while saying the Creed. She reminds me of the writer Rose Macaulay, who was able to hold Faith and Doubt in her heart

simultaneously. That is an essential ingredient of anything Ysenda Maxtone Graham writes. In the middle
of laughing, you often find yourself having a serious
thought, or with tears in your eyes.

She is especially sympathetic to the hermit-like
retired headmaster David Atkinson, who stepped down
in 1989 and who would not be interviewed for the
book. She describes how he flatly refused to have a
retirement party and threw almost all his belongings,
including precious souvenirs, into a builder's skip
before disappearing for good to the country. His joint-
headmaster was a young visionary teacher, Harry
Biggs-Davison, who took over the headship and has
transformed the school into a place of true educational
excellence.

Let us end with a truly Maxtone Grahamish piece of
trivia which no one else would have bothered to record.
We are looking where we are not meant to go – in
David Atkinson's private engagement diary.

Harry remembers one particular diary entry
which gave him new insight into the private
habits of his co-headmaster.

'I was trying to fix up a late-afternoon interview
with some parents, and saw that David had written in the diary, "5 p.m.: S.T. 6 p.m.: R.F." I told

him I wanted to see some parents in the office but had noticed that he'd booked appointments for those times. "Oh, no, no, no," David said, slightly embarrassed. "Those aren't appointments. They're just something private."'

Whom could the initials 'S.T.' and 'R.F.' stand for, Harry wondered? He was intrigued. It wasn't until later, when he was flicking through the *Radio Times*, that he spotted '5.00: *Star Trek*' and '6.00: *The Rockford Files*.'

If you see the poignancy, and the high comedy of this revelation, then not only will you hugely enjoy *Mr Tibbits's Catholic School*; you will have been welcomed into the Ysenda Maxtone Graham world, and the smile will never quite leave your face.

A. N. WILSON

Introduction

'Wasn't that old Dick Tibbits's place?'

Those words will haunt me for ever. They were spoken to me over the telephone on 9 December 2009 by the 86-year-old Earl of Gainsborough. He was one of the four knobbly-kneed boys in the first St Philip's School photograph, taken in 1934.

'Yes, that's right. I'm writing a history of the school, and I'd love to ask you about your memories of it.'

The Earl was speaking to me from his house in Rutland. 'Well, I do come to London occasionally. In fact, I'm coming up next week. I always stay at the Sloane Club.'

'That's wonderful! Can I come and see you?'

'I'm afraid I'm going to be rather busy. Lots of things going on. It might be difficult to fit you in.'

'Are you sure you haven't got a spare half-hour? It wouldn't take long.'

'Mmm. I'm very sorry, but I'm afraid not. I'll be up

again early in the New Year, though. I'll see you then. Goodbye.'

'Look forward to it! Goodbye.'

On 11 January I rang the house in Rutland to enquire whether another London visit was imminent. There was no reply. On 25 January I rang the Earl's nephew Robert Noel. He told me that his uncle had been 'harvested' in the cold snap. A requiem was to be held for him at the Oratory in three days' time.

*

The ongoing tragedy of the Passing of Time, which we all have to live through and get used to, came home to me countless times while researching the history of St Philip's. Just reading every school magazine from 1968 (when the magazines started) to the present day made me see with appalling clarity the fleetingness of childhood. A little boy is mentioned in the list of New Boys; a few issues later he wins a prize in the art competition; then you see his name again, the byline for an essay called 'A Visit to the Zoo' or 'My Ideal Island'. A few issues later, he's mentioned in dispatches of Colts matches; then of First XI matches; then (if he's a star pupil) as 'Squad commander' or winner of the History Cup; and then as a leaver. It's all over. The Venerable Bede's Anglo-Saxon allegory of a sparrow flying into a fire-lit feasting hall and out again at the other end into the dark winter came constantly to mind.

But my encounter with the Earl of Gainsborough took the biscuit, with regard to shocking reminders of mortality.

All I had from him were those six words: 'Wasn't that old Dick Tibbits's place?' I comforted myself with the thought that if he was asking that question, rather than saying, 'Oh, yes, that was old Dick Tibbits's place', perhaps he would have been a bit vague anyway. But I got something from those six words that no other St Philip's old boy had given me. He was the only one I met who referred to his old headmaster as 'Dick'. Was it a perk of being an aged earl, I wondered, that he could refer to his prep-school headmaster in such a casual way?

*

When I suggested to Harry Biggs-Davison that I might write a history of St Philip's, he was delighted, and instantly helpful. He himself had been a new boy at the school in 1963. What he longed to know more about, he told me, were the early days, from the school's opening in 1934 until the early 1960s. The aforementioned Richard Tibbits, its founder, 'kept not a single piece of paper', Harry told me. 'No accounts or files. He kept everything in his head. I'd love to know more about the early days. I'm worried that so much history will be lost for ever when our oldest old boys die.'

So, as I began researching, I found myself mentally grading old boys and teachers in this order:

2000s: hardly worth talking to, because not yet history

1990s: possibly a quick chat

1980s: worth talking to

1970s: getting a bit more interesting

1960s: even more interesting

1950s: fascinating

1940s: enthralling

1930s: utterly engrossing. Pre-war boys are gold-dust.

Sitting in the school office on Day One as the school's historian, I was given the bald facts. They are these. In the early 1930s Father Talbot of the Oratory had a chat with Richard Tibbits, a Catholic convert and schoolmaster, and told him that South Kensington was in need of a Catholic prep-school.

Mr Tibbits bought 6 Wetherby Place and started St Philip's in September 1934 with four pupils. He used to collect them from their houses in the morning and drive them to school, and then drive them home again in the afternoon. By 1936 there were sixteen boys, and by 1939 there were twenty-seven.

When war broke out, Mr Tibbits took a small group of St Philip's boys to Warwick with him for a year. Then he joined the Army and was away for the rest of the war. The school was completely shut up during the war years.

It wasn't bombed, but the house opposite was destroyed.

Mr Tibbits married Muriel Atkinson in 1946, and re-opened the school in 1947. Mrs Tibbits became the school housekeeper until her retirement in 1984.

Mr Tibbits died of a heart attack in 1967. His wife's nephew David Atkinson, a master at the school, took over as headmaster. He was an Anglican, as was his aunt Mrs Tibbits. The school's connection with the Oratory broke off for twenty-three years. Father Patrick Keely of the Carmelite Church in Kensington became the school's chaplain. Mrs Tibbits was given a Papal *Bene Merenti* medal by Cardinal Hume in 1983 for carrying on running St Philip's as a Catholic school.

(Here's a poem about that, which was published in the school magazine in 1983:

Ave, Ave, Tibbite, receivis gold medallion!
Pontifexi down the roadi stixit on lapellium.

Bene-very-much-merenti, de te sumus proudii:
Multos annos putting up cum Catholici loudii.

The author of that? The great science master Roger
Taylor, of whom more anon.)

Mr Atkinson was sole headmaster for eighteen years,
until 1984, when Harry Biggs-Davison became joint
headmaster with him. This arrangement lasted until
1989, when Mr Atkinson retired from being headmaster (but carried on being a history master till 1998).
Harry Biggs-Davison became headmaster, which he
remains to this day.

*

As you'll have noticed, reading these introductory
paragraphs, the name 'Tibbits' – not a particularly
attractive or poetic surname in itself – is spoken in
every other breath when recounting the history of the
school. You're probably getting quite tired of the name
already, and I've only just begun. What's more, the
school's kitchen-maid in the 1970s, Cissy, could never
get her employer's name right, though she worked for
her, both as school maid and domestic daily help, for
years. She always called her 'Mrs Tippit'. Here is a
typical snatch of conversation between them.

'Well, Cissy, what do you think we shall have for
luncheon today?'

'I dunno, Mrs Tippit.'

'What about luncheon meat?'

'Oh, good idea, Mrs Tippit.'

'And what vegetables shall we have, Cissy?'

'What about mash, Mrs Tippit?'

'Good idea, Cissy. Mashed potatoes it is! And I think we might have some Russian salad as well.'

The absurd thing about this regular exchange, as the school's art teacher Denise Bolam told me, was that the menu was a foregone conclusion. Lunches were on a seven-day cycle. If it was Tuesday, it was spam and mash. But Mrs Tibbits – and Cissy, too – enjoyed entertaining the illusion of choice and spontaneity.

I came out of my first briefing in the school office with the T-word ringing in my head. Harry had shown me a photograph of the man during his Army days: an imposing face with small eyes. The curvature of the lips suggested that his voice was as military as his uniform.

I was soon to discover that, though Mr Tibbits named the school 'St Philip's' (after St Philip Neri, founder of the first Oratory in Rome in 1556), it was always referred to by boys and teachers as 'Tibbits' until his death. So much was the man the school, and the school the man.

I also came out of the office that day weighed down with Box One of the complete *Three Stars* editions. The first issue of the school magazine (named after the three stars on St Philip Neri's coat of arms) came out in March 1968, typed on sheets of foolscap paper, duplicated and stapled. 'We boys stapled these together ourselves,' Harry Biggs-Davison said. 'Mr Atkinson made the *Three Stars* crest by gouging out a rubber with a razor blade.'

'The editor hopes [ran the Editorial of Issue Number 1] that before long the *Three Stars* will become a real part of school life, like Box Hill, Mark Reading, and visiting the zoo on Shrove Tuesday.'

What, or who, I wondered, was Mark Reading? Was it (or he) (a) the tradition of reading aloud the Gospel according to St Mark; (b) a well-known St Philip's boy whose surname was pronounced like the Berkshire town; or (c) something to do with reading out boys' school marks? I longed to find out.

*

It's a bit weird, I admit, to be so fascinated by such a question. What does it matter what (or who) Mark Reading was? Are prep schools all that interesting?

I would argue that they are. The years from 7 to 13 shape the rest of our lives in ways too deep for words. Over the course of five months I would interview scores of St Philip's old boys, from every vintage. It was astonishing how vividly they remembered their prep-school days. A few of the very old ones had Alzheimer's and would tell me the same things again and again ('Mr Tibbits did have quite a temper'). But each of them had a handful of shiningly detailed recollections which they had carried with them from boyhood, and which seemed to have shaped and informed the rest of their lives. Many of them had a certain foodstuff they had avoided for half a century, after being made to eat it at St Philip's.

I kept wondering what it would be like if someone were interviewing me about my time at Sibton Park Preparatory School for girls in the early 1970s. Yes, I could certainly still tell you what we had for lunch on each day of the week. Monday will always be a mince-coloured day in my mind. We remember those days as if they were yesterday: the feel of the itchy uniform, the smell of the dining-room, the taste of the mash, the voices of the teachers, the names, faces and habits of the other pupils, the feeling of being loved or hated. The hilarious moments, and the traumatic moments, stay with us for ever. The years from 7 to 13 seem to be particularly formative. We are young enough to be innocent and impressionable, yet old enough to think and feel deeply about what is happening to us.

St Philip's seems to exert a particularly strong influence

on anybody who has anything to do with it. Anyone who is or has been a mother there (let alone a boy) knows this feeling. As soon as your son starts at the bottom of the school, you live in dread of the moment when he'll leave. How will you manage not to sink into depression without the devouring of the weekly newsletter, the thrill of a White Shirt Day, the sight of 110 boys in blazers the colour of St Philip Neri's shield filing in to the Little Oratory for Mass on a weekday morning? Mothers have been known to have extra 'afterthought' sons just in order to prolong the St Philip's experience. Most of all I envy Nicola Roberts, whose seven sons Sebastian, Nicholas, Hilarion, Cassian, Lucian, Fabian and Damian all went there. She was granted a long, long sojourn in the warm feasting hall before having to fly out again into the dark.

Countless people I have spoken to talk of the family feel of the school. London has become a bewildering place for private-school-seeking parents. Where do you go, and how do you get in? At one end of the spectrum are the hothouses, where (one hears) 'nothing your child does is good enough'. At the other end are the wishy-washy, education-shirking schools where whole terms are devoted to a project on the Chinese New Year. At crowded 'open mornings' at vast, money-raking 'chain' schools, you are shown round in groups and are expected to be dazzled by the gleaming facilities, whereas in truth your eyes are beginning to glaze over at the very words 'refurbished ICT suite'.

Then (if you still haven't found what you're looking for), you might ring St Philip's. Mrs Rennie answers. She is the niece of the great Mrs Tolmie who taught at the school for many years, a thick-ankled legend of whom (again) more anon. A fortnight later you find yourself being shown round individually by the headmaster.

This is a vital moment. As you look round the school, you come face to face with your priorities. If you're the kind of person who can't stand narrow corridors, steep staircases, crucifixes, pictures of the Pope, and a garden without a football goal, you'll quickly realize that this school is not for you. Though you may not know it, you're experiencing the school's own built-in filtering mechanism.

But if there's something about the atmosphere of the place that warms your heart, in spite of (or even because of) the school's size, you might inadvertently have got through the filter. ICT suites and indoor swimming-pools just don't cut the mustard for the kind of parent you've discovered you are. What you are after is the rare mixture of good education, a nurturing atmosphere, fun and soul.

Marius Barran remembers thinking, on his first day at the school in 1957, 'I can't believe you can fit 100 boys into this house which is smaller than our family house in Kensington.'

But you can.

*

And so I set out, armed with nothing but the Bald Facts. Phrases from the Bald Facts kept going round in my head. I longed to make them less bald. 'Mr Tibbits took some boys to Warwick with him at the beginning of the War.' Why Warwick? Where in Warwick? What was it like in Warwick? Was anybody still alive who went to Warwick with Mr Tibbits?

On the very day that I managed to track down a boy who had actually been one of the Warwick Seven, the first episode of the new Radio 4 series *A History of the World in 100 Objects* was broadcast. I felt (absurdly, perhaps) a similar frisson speaking to the Warwick old boy, as if I were holding the 2-million-year-old hand-axe from the Olduvai Gorge in Tanzania. 'Why get so excited?' you might ask. It was only an old man who went to Warwick during the war. Well, it was only a hand-axe. But the past is the past, whether 60 years ago or 2 million years ago. If it's lost it's gone for ever.

This book could almost be called 'A History of St Philip's in 100 Cups of Coffee'. Whenever possible I interviewed people in the flesh, rather than on the telephone. It was fascinating to see what they looked like, and what kind of life they'd made for themselves. (In general, the news is good. Take, for example, Edward Leigh, MP, whom I came across, early on the first morning of the Cameron-Clegg coalition, taking a dip in the Serpentine in old clingy nylon trunks. A heartening sight.) I've sampled every kind of coffee, from Nescafé, through filter and cafetière, to the finest whisked cappuccino, at the houses of old boys and old teachers. The French teacher Stephen de la Bedoyère's instant coffee with malt loaf in his 1930s mansion flat in Balham stands out, as does coffee and thin biscuits in Edward Coventry's unlived-in drawing-room in Barnes, as he gave me new insights into school swimming lessons in the 1950s.

Having written a book on the Church of England, I can tell you that St Philip's old boys compare favourably to Church of England vicars in two ways. First, their coffee is better (stronger and less milky). Second, they answer their own telephones and can generally find a time to talk to you within the next ten

days. I came across hardly any pomposity in all my researches.

There was only one person who declined to talk to me, and he was a pivotal person. David Atkinson, who was headmaster of the school from 1967 to 1990, wrote me the following from his home on the South Coast.

> I regret I cannot receive visitors, neither do I possess a computer or any modern gadgets; also phoning is no use (usually) as I cannot stand daily nuisance calls so don't answer. Therefore, mail permitting, I can only be contacted by letter.

In short, he's a recluse. Everyone says so. Even his old colleagues who love him dearly never see him. They just have an occasional exchange of Christmas cards.

But old boys remember him with enormous fondness. I'm hoping that in these pages his character and traits will be strongly illuminated through people's memories of him. After reading those words from him, I did contact him by letter, asking him ten written questions. When, a month later, he still hadn't replied, I brazenly picked up the telephone (his bracketed word 'usually' gave me a glimmer of hope) and dialled his Sussex number. His telephone rang and rang. I imagined him sitting by it, fuming at the modern age with these nuisance callers who ring you from call centres trying to sell you something. It was too cruel. After fifteen rings I hung up.

As you live through the school's story in these chapters you'll be taken on a meander through the twentieth century. War, rationing, smog, mini-skirts, maxi-skirts, strikes, Thatcherism, the first computer: you will encounter them all through the lens of a small Catholic prep school in South Kensington.

I

Pre-War Boys

It was a bit like going to have a chat with Winston Churchill. I could hardly see the Hon. Gerard Noel for the cigar smoke. It was ten in the morning and we sat in his little study in his mansion flat near Sloane Square. Through the fug, his wife appeared with cups of coffee. Eyes watering, I thanked her. At last, I was face to face with a Pre-War Boy.

Gerard Noel is the younger brother of the Earl of Gainsborough (who still had a month or so to live, at the time of this meeting). Gerard was born in 1926, and went to St Philip's in 1937 for two years until the outbreak of the war.

Every St Philip's old boy I met who had been at the school under Mr Tibbits gave me a new adjective or a new insight into the man's appearance and character. Animals were often used for comparison: a pig, a whale, a hippopotamus. I came across a whole thesaurus's-worth of synonyms for 'fat' while listening to descriptions of Mr Tibbits. Again and again I was told of the same dichotomy: extreme strictness and loss of temper on occasions, mixed with the deepest kindness, compassion and care for the forming of boys' minds and souls.

'A dumpy, untidy, erratic man,' Gerard Noel said. 'Always a cigarette hanging out of his mouth, and always spilling the ash.' (This from a man whose own cigar ash was in need of a firm flick against an ashtray.) 'But he was a genius at teaching. A born schoolmaster. He used to line us up against the wall of the classroom and fire general knowledge questions at us: "What's the capital of . . ." and so on. When we were writing he'd walk round the room and lean over our desks, making corrections as we were working. He was a particularly good teacher of religion. The way he described Communion, the Real Presence . . . he made us devout, he made us love going to church.'

And then, 'He could be very peppery. He used to hold the bottom of his coat and *shake* with anger.'

*

Richard H. Tibbits was born in 1903 in Warwick and was a convert to Catholicism. He was educated at Epsom College and at The Queen's College, Oxford. The Queen's College archivist informed me that the 'H' stood for 'Harman', and that he came away with a Third in History. When he started at Oxford he was still firmly Church of England. 'Hopes to be ordained,' wrote the Provost of the college in his notes. Tibbits's conversion took place while he was at Oxford. After he left, he taught for nine years at St Anthony's, Eastbourne, where he was assistant master. His favourite place of worship was the home of Catholic converts, the London Oratory. One day, chatting after Mass to an Oratory Father, he had the conversation that sparked the founding of St Philip's. Something like this:

> Father Talbot of the Oratory: 'Dick, we really could do with a boys' Catholic prep school in the area.'
> R.T.: 'Good idea. Would you like me to start one?'
> Fr T.: 'Yes, please do.'
> R.T.: 'All right.'

Thirty-four years after this exchange, on 20 October 1978, Harry Biggs-Davison conducted an interview with Mrs Tibbits, which he recorded on a cassette. He transcribed the whole interview, and this typed document is one of the very few sources for the school's beginnings. Here is Mrs Tibbits on Richard Tibbits's reply to Father Talbot:

> Dick said all right and he went about looking for houses and found one. Well, then, he started the

school off and his sister Betty Tibbits came and did the housekeeping.

It all sounds extremely easy. No mention of putting in an offer, finding the money to afford a whole house in sw7, or getting it ready to be a school. Just 'he went about looking for houses and found one'. The house was 6 Wetherby Place.

('Oh, yes, I remember Mr Tibbits's sister,' Gerard Noel told me. 'She was terrifying. Very strict and not popular with the boys. She stood over us and made us eat our rice pudding. Very efficient, though.')

But what was it that prompted Father Talbot to say, 'we really could do with a boys' Catholic prep school in the area?' Louis Jebb, great-grandson of Hilaire Belloc and nephew of Francis and Patrick Pollen, two of the earliest pupils at the school, gave me an inkling. He described to me a world of smart Catholic mothers in the 1930s who went to the Oratory each Sunday, and who cared about getting a good Catholic education for their sons – and their daughters. 'My grandmother Daphne Pollen was active in starting More House, a Catholic school for girls, in 1952,' Louis Jebb told me. 'That was more than fifteen years later; but it shows that mothers were concerned about this sort of thing. These women were thick with the Oratorians.'

In September 1934 the school opened, with four pupils. The opening of the school is mentioned in the Oratory's minutes: 'At a General Congregation on the 20th March [1935], it was unanimously agreed to give our patronage to a Catholic preparatory school for boys, to be opened by Mr R. Tibbits in Wetherby Place.' The number of pupils rose quickly to eleven. The next picture you have to have in your head, while imagining this dawn of the school, is of Mr Tibbits (who, still a bachelor, had set up a little flat for himself at the top of the house) driving off at 7.45 each morning to collect his pupils.

For details of this daily school run, we have the written testimony of Richard Harvey, another pre-war boy, who described his memories in a letter written to Harry Biggs-Davison from Australia in 1999.

Tibbits would head off from Wetherby Place each school-day morning in his large beige tourer, a Humber *circa* 1929, I think. Fairly frequently in wet weather he had to resort to the crank, and both he and the car seemed to have their tempers aroused, one popping, banging and emitting clouds of smoke, the other getting increasingly red in the face, to say nothing of the 'utterings'.

The first pick-up was O'Gorman from Prince

of Wales Road overlooking Battersea Park. From there he would re-cross the Thames and go up to the corner of Bywater Street where I would be waiting. Next stop was Upper Belgrave Street, where Bertie [surname, pronounced 'Bartie'] was loaded on board, then off we went to Park Lane to collect Gainsborough and his brother Noel. Lastly Ennismore Gardens to collect Lowndes.

In the afternoon the whole process would be repeated in reverse. It was a novel way of recruiting families to a new school: to offer to be both headmaster and chauffeur.

Being driven by Mr Tibbits seems to be a powerful memory for many old boys. Cars in the 1930s were exciting things in themselves; and the experience of getting into your headmaster's car helped you to see the human side of him, in the days when schoolmasters were a lofty breed whom it was hard to believe actually had a life of their own. I've heard Mr Tibbits's car described countless times: 'a square box on wheels', 'a ramshackle car', 'a canvas-topped thing', 'a poor man's Rolls', 'something of an old banger', 'we called it the boneshaker' – and always full of boys, piled into the back without safety belts. He also drove boys to cricket matches, or to visit Downside or Worth if they were thinking of going there.

But Gerard Noel alerted me to the 'rival car' in the 1930s: a boy called Paul Wright was brought to school in his family's much grander vehicle, 'the Maroon Pontiac'.

Looking through his grandmother Daphne Pollen's diary for 1935, Louis Jebb found the following entries, which give a rosy picture of her two sons' early days at the school:

> 16 May 1935: Went to see new Papist prep school for boys.
> 11 September: Bought boys' school outfits at Rowe.
> 23 September: Boys' first day at Mr Tibbits's school. Back for lunch. Cecilia [the boys' 5-year-old sister] said, 'Now we'll have a lot of chatter' when she heard them at the door.
> 24 September: Boys still thrilled by school.

(Her use of the word 'Papist' struck me as odd. The dictionary definition of 'Papist' is 'a disparaging term for a Catholic'. I asked Louis Jebb if he thought there were any dark undertones in his grandmother's use of this word in her diary, but he assured me there weren't. She, herself a convert, used the term simply to mean Catholic and Pope-following.)

There were only two masters at the beginning of the school's life: Mr Tibbits and 'Bunny' Newall. What was

'Bunny' Newall like? 'Serious, but we liked him,' Gerard Noel remembers. Mrs Tibbits, on the recorded cassette, remembers differently (although her 'memories' are in fact hearsay from her husband, as she was not married to Mr Tibbits at the time). 'Bunny was a dreadful man, a boozer of the worst sort, and he used to come in at eleven crawling on hands and feet upstairs and blundering about the place; and in the end Bunny had to go. The last I heard of him he was propping up a long bar in Shanghai.'

This description tells us as much about Mrs Tibbits as it does about 'Bunny' Newall. One wonders what her definition of 'a boozer of the best sort' would be. Either she liked someone, or she didn't. If she didn't, she wrote them off with a few terse, scathing words. 'Tiresome' was one of her favourites, along with 'a mere cipher' and 'wet as a wonk'.

'We had a very good gym instructor who'd been in the Navy,' Gerard Noel said,

and a singing teacher called Miss Mason who taught us hymns. 'Don't sing "Amen" at the end: it's very Protestant,' she'd tell us. Miss Vacani used to send a lady to give us boys dancing lessons. Sometimes a couple called the Kenworthy-Browns came from another school to teach us catechism. Reading the Bible we came across the word 'sodomy' and asked Mrs Kenworthy-Brown what it meant. 'Oh, don't worry about that,' she told us. 'You'll be doing that next year with Mr Kenworthy-Brown.'

(This, I suspect, is an anecdote that Gerard Noel has dined out on for over seventy years.)

He remembers Mr Tibbits taking the boys for long walks round London to look at buildings, and up to Kensington Gardens to play football. 'And he took us to confession once every three weeks. He used to say, "Every week is too often, every month is not enough".'

'When I'd been at the school for a year,' Gerard Noel said, 'Tibbits got a new teacher, Hugh Barrett-Lennard, who became one of the great influences of my life.'

Barrett-Leonard (later Father Sir Hugh Barrett-Lennard, Bt.), who died in 2007 aged 89, was to become one of the most loved and most eccentric Oratory Fathers, famous for wearing mismatched shoes and getting his cassock caught in his bicycle wheel. Picture him being asked for confession by a female parishioner on the front steps of the Oratory, and holding up his tennis racket as a grille so that the separation between confessor and penitent could be maintained.

'When he started at St Philip's he was 22 and had just become a Catholic,' Gerard Noel said.

> He was quite uninhibited as a teacher. He would act out parts of Ovid and Homer, and would rush up and down the classroom declaiming the words. He was an imaginative teacher – he did things like organizing debates for us boys. I must have been very well taught. When I got to my school in America during the war, I was quite easily top of the class.

*

Gerard Noel's study was a smoky blur when I left; but in exchange I'd gained some crystal-sharp insights into those pre-war days. His abiding memory was of happiness. 'A very balanced school, all sort of normal, quite informal. It was like a family, really.'

Nowadays we expect schools to be happy places, but in those days pupil enjoyment was low on the list of most schools' priorities. The pre-war Tibbits seems to have been a gentle man as well as a gentleman: he cared about his boys, he wanted to mould their minds and their souls, and he only rarely lost his temper – as often with his car as with his pupils.

In later pages of this book we'll see him as a more irascible man, ardent with the slipper. During the war, something changed in his character. But for now, he's a man any boy would be happy to sit next to at lunch.

'But he used to get ever so cross occasionally.'

This was Michael Lowndes, another pre-war boy, talking to me at his house in Ealing. He repeated that several times. And, desperate as I was for more detailed insights from hard-to-track-down pre-war boys, Michael Lowndes was a slightly unforthcoming interviewee.

'Do you remember the food?'

'It was normal, perfectly satisfactory, nothing particularly remarkable.'

'What was Mr Tibbits like?'

'Very pleasant. Always very pleasant. But he could get very cross sometimes.'

'Can you remember anything he taught you?'

'I think he taught everything, really, in those days.'

'What was Hugh Barrett-Lennard like?'

'A very nice man, very friendly. One could talk to him.'

'Has the building changed much since you were there in the 1930s?'

'It's pretty much the same, really.'

And so on. The only two detailed vignettes he gave

me were these: 'Mr Tibbits used to take us to cricket matches at Lord's, which meant a whole day off school'; and 'Once, Mr Tibbits's car broke down just after he'd dropped me off at 68 Ennismore Gardens, and the boys all came into my house. We had a staff of three in those days: a cook, a parlourmaid, and an ordinary maid.'

He remembered the breaks from normality rather than the normality.

Michael Lowndes's life has been clouded by one appalling event. He was involved in the Downside tragedy of 1943, in which his brother David (who had also briefly been at St Philip's) was killed. During a cricket match on a balmy July afternoon, two fighter planes were flying above the cricket ground during a flying lesson. 'We were all sitting on a grassy bank watching the cricket match, or, in my case, reading,' Michael Lowndes told me. 'The learner was trying to be clever. He flew low, caught his wing on a branch, and crashed. His plane burst into flames. Nine boys were killed, including my brother, and nine or ten of us were in hospital. I was in hospital for months with burns.'

It's not surprising, perhaps, that most of the smaller details of St Philip's daily life have been lost to his memory.

*

'When war broke out, Mr Tibbits took a few boys to Warwick for a year.'

This is the much-heard sentence we now need to flesh out. The day must have come, in September 1939, when Mr Tibbits locked the front door of 6 Wetherby Place, little knowing that he would not return to it for seven years. Here is Mrs Tibbits on the subject, ever-sweeping, ever-vague.

HBD: 'What happened when the war came?'
MT: 'Well, he had to go. Dick's mother lived in a large house [in Warwick]. His father was a doctor. They had a huge house and tons of rooms, so Dick suggested to parents that he would take any boys there who wanted to go on going to school, and he arranged to go to a local prep school for lessons. So he used to march off with them after breakfast in the morning.'

To corroborate this, we have the detailed memories of Christopher Campbell-Johnston, father of Rachel *The Times* art critic and brother of Michael the Jesuit priest in Barbados. Christopher spoke to me from his home in Droitwich, his wife by his side helping him and encouraging him to remember.

I was born in 1933 so I was 6 when we went to

Warwick, and my brother was $7\frac{1}{2}$. Seven of us boys went, in two cars: the hard core of the school. We stayed in Mr Tibbits's family's house, a splendid house half-way up the hill on the High Street. We took our nanny with us. She came and looked after us and after all the boys. We just called her 'Nanny', but her real name was Beatrice Jeffries. She was very kind and gentle but would-n't stand for any nonsense. I still keep a photo-graph of her on my chest of drawers. You see a gentle kindness in her face, like a calm sea.

Their nanny went with them! This was a riveting new detail. You can imagine them all in this large house in Warwick High Street, the boys sleeping in iron beds with dipping mattresses, Beatrice Jeffries tucking them up before lights-out. 'Our ages ranged from 6 to 11. Shaun McAndrews and an Italian boy called Corsi were the eldest. Laver was another. Often at night-time you heard boys crying in their beds. It was quite often that I cried, too.'

Were Mr Tibbits's parents there? 'His father had died, but his mother was there. She tried to keep well out of the way. We were extremely badly behaved and ill-disciplined. I seem to remember that his mother died within a short while of us getting there.'

Where did they go to school while they were in Warwick? 'Arnold something,' Christopher Campbell-Johnston told me. 'Arnold's School? Arnold House?' 'What was it called?' His wife coaxed him to remember. 'Arnold LODGE. That was it. It was in Leamington Spa. Mr Tibbits drove us there every morning.' (Cue description of car.) 'He had the oldest and most cranky car you can imagine, a box on four wheels, I think a Morris 8. We climbed into it by the steps of the house each morning. It never started. On a nice icy day you'd see all seven of us pushing like hell.'

Arnold Lodge is still going strong, and has a website. 'The only independent school in South Warwickshire educating girls and boys from kindergarten to GCSE... Every child at Arnold Lodge is recognized as an individual with different experiences, aptitudes and capabilities.' The usual website stuff. The only subject glaringly missing from the curriculum (Mr Tibbits would not approve) is Latin. I rang the school secretary to ask if she knew of a retired teacher who might remember seven Roman Catholic London evacuees coming to the school during the war, and she forwarded an e-mail from me to the old headmaster Mr Hall, but nothing more was heard.

'We being stinkers rather turned our noses up at the dropped aitches,' Christopher Campbell-Johnston remembers. 'We didn't much like the school. We considered ourselves a cut above.'

'What was Mr Tibbits like when he was in Warwick?'

(Cue animal imagery and words for 'fat'.)

'Well, he had a number of features which made him pig-like. He made one think of a Beatrix Potter drawing: a very nice old pig. There was plenty of spare flesh wherever you looked. But he was a very kind and good man.'

There's still a firm of solicitors in Warwick High Street called Moore & Tibbits. I rang them and asked to speak to Mr Tibbits (hoping for a current family member) but was told that no actual Tibbits had worked at the firm for over a hundred years.

Mr Tibbits's younger brother Dr Stephen Tibbits got a warm obituary in the *British Medical Journal* of December 1979. 'During 44 years of medical service to the inhabitants of Warwick he became the best-known and most universally loved character in the town. He was a portly, almost Dickensian figure . . .'

So it turns out that there were two portly Tibbits brothers, one a pillar of St Mary's Anglican church in Warwick, and the other a pillar of the Oratory in London.

*

A year into the war, 'Dick got the fidgets and wanted to join up, and so he went and joined up, and then he went into the Army and went through the war and all that.'

Thus spoke (you probably recognize the voice by now) Mrs Tibbits into the tape recorder. 'Finally he landed in the Guards Armoured Division as education officer under that awful man Wigg, the most loathsome man Dick ever met.'

'That awful man Wigg' was George Wigg, who was to become the Labour MP for Dudley in the 1945 General Election, and who later used parliamentary procedure to put John Profumo's affair with Christine Keeler on record in *Hansard*, which sparked the scandal leading to Profumo's eventual resignation. Mr Tibbits hated Wigg during the war mainly because he went around giving lectures telling people to vote Labour, when the lectures he was giving were supposed to be apolitical. 'A most loathsome bit of work,' Mrs Tibbits says on the tape.

Then she cuts straight to 'Well, finally Dick got demobbed; he got to colonel.' Her husband's war years are fleetingly glossed over. Was it true, as Kevin Pakenham told me having been told it himself, that Lieutenant-Colonel Richard Tibbits was among the first members of the British Army who went into the concentration camps in 1945? In order to verify this by checking his service records, I needed permission from his next-of-kin. To ask who this might be I wrote, again, to Mrs Tibbits's nephew, the reclusive David Atkinson. In reply I received a 1970s postcard of the Polperro Horse Bus, on the back of which was written, 'Re your letter and card regret have been in bed on and off with 'flu so cannot answer letters etc. Better perhaps in spring. D.R.A.' Spring came and went without a word.

After being demobbed, Mr Tibbits taught at Worth for a year, before the time came to re-open St Philip's. And in the two years after the end of the war, his romance with the future Mrs Tibbits blossomed.

2

Mr Tibbits in Love

Muriel MacFarlane was a widow when she and Mr Tibbits fell in love. Her late husband, Wing-Commander MacFarlane, had died from injuries received in the Quetta Earthquake in Baluchistan in 1935, which killed 40,000 people. For her work in helping the survivors of the earthquake, she was awarded the Kaisar-i-Hind medal by the Indian Government. For the rest of her life, she always wore her first husband's flying wings, a little brooch on her lapel.

She had lost a brother in the First World War. In 1940, her only son was shot down and killed over Dieppe. Her life had been dogged by tragedy. But she herself seems to have been a remarkably un-tragic person. Her reaction to tragedy was to keep busy. At her memorial service in 1986, Roger Taylor (who gave the address) mentioned the death of her son. 'So what did Mrs Tibbits do? She threw herself into war work with the American Red Cross. We can all picture her telling some enormous GI not to be so wet, and that a little daylight bombing would do him the world of good.'

He also said, 'She was always known as "Mrs Tibbits". Even now, it would be a very rash seraphim, or cheeky cherub, who would attempt to be more familiar. St Peter himself will have to write "Mrs Tibbits" – no more, no less – in his book.'

Her lack of sentimentality and of self-pity mani-fested themselves in a briskness of manner and an avoidance of emotional vocabulary. Thus, when Harry Biggs-Davison asked her on the 1978 cassette how she and Mr Tibbits got together, the word 'love' did not come into her answer.

The two of them had met briefly before the war, she told him, at Aldro School in Surrey, where her son (whose name was Ruthven, though he was always known as 'Bim') was at school. Her sister Audrey was joint owner and matron. Mr Tibbits was a master at St Anthony's, Eastbourne, at the time and had visited Aldro and got to know some of the boys. 'You must meet Mr Tibbits,' Bim had said to his mother. 'He's the most marvellous man. I wish he was a master here.' 'Well, one Sunday there was a supper party with all sorts of people, and Tibbs was there. Tibbs, they called him. So I was introduced, and I said, "I've heard about you from my son." "Oh, yes," he said, "He's a great friend of mine." Then I never saw him again at all.'

Mrs Tibbits proceeds, on the cassette, to dash briskly and brusquely through her own war years. 'In 1940 my son was killed and in 1942 my husband died. So that had me stranded.'

She worked in the canteen at Taunton for the American Red Cross until the troops left for D-Day. Then she went back to Aldro to help her sister look after the house. Mr Tibbits visited the school while on leave and Audrey, who had flu, said to her, 'Tibbs is coming, so please will you look after him?'

'So I had to look after Tibbs, and that led to the thing. It took me a long time, though.'

'That led to the thing.' A tantalizing glimpse of their burgeoning romance, and all we have to go on. Their courtship seems to have been a slow-burning business. One of the things they did during it was to go and look at 6 Wetherby Place, which had been shut up since 1939. 'Well, I'm not going to marry you and go and live in a place like this,' was Muriel's reaction. 'I couldn't stand it. It was awful. I can't tell you how filthy.'

In 1947 they were married by Abbot Farwell OSB of Downside. Mrs Tibbits was, and remained, an Anglican.

Her father had given her a stern piece of advice: 'Don't marry a Catholic or a teacher.'

*

St Philip's had stood dark and empty since 1939, gathering Blitz dust. The flying bomb that had destroyed the house opposite in 1944 had left 6 Wetherby Place unscathed apart from a few broken windows. 'In that space,' Mrs Tibbits said in the taped interview, pointing across the road, 'the old woman and her maid who would not evacuate were blown to bits by the bomb.'

Nothing had changed inside the building. 'When Dick came back he found even the gas fires all here. I said, "How are we ever going to get it clean?" He said, "Well the Government are going to do some painting." Well, they did painting, though it all peeled off in about two weeks. We started off in 1947.'

Thus began the unbroken run of school-term routine at St Philip's which continues to this day. Games twice a week, swimming once a week, Mass three or four times a term: thus it was then and thus it still is now.

Mr and Mrs Tibbits made a flat for themselves to live in at the top of the house. Mr Tibbits asked his sister (the 'terrifying' woman remembered by Gerard Noel) whether she'd like to come back and help at the school but she said, No, thank you, she'd rather be in Warwick. 'She was a rather tiresome spin, you know,' said Mrs Tibbits. (One more character curtly written off.)

'We started with about twenty boys,' she continued, 'and in those days it was difficult because the place was full of Polish refugees and there was a Polish Association who kept bothering us to take them for nothing. Well, we took as many as we could for nothing, but we couldn't go on taking them for nothing, or for about ten pounds a term. A little school like us couldn't be responsible for a lot of Poles. Well, soon the Poles sort of filtered out, and we got known round about, and then we began getting the Catholic boys. It started from there.'

*

There are a few things you are going to have to get used to, as you read the forthcoming pages. You will come across certain traits which to us in the twenty-first century seem unattractive, if not downright shocking. The important thing to point out is that they were quite normal in those days. They didn't just happen at St Philip's with the Tibbitses. They happened at nearly all prep schools. The traits are these:

Lots of the teachers smoked. Not just a little: all the time, so that their fingers were yellow and the whole place stank of stale ash.

Most of the male teachers drank quite a lot, heading straight for the nearest pub after school hours.

The boys got beaten with a slipper. Pants down, bend over: the whole thing.

There was mild xenophobia in the air (as exemplified by Mrs Tibbits's slightly disdainful way of referring, above, to 'a lot of Poles').

Christopher Gardner-Thorpe, who was at St Philip's from 1948 to 1954, arranged to meet me in the lounge of the Hilton near Paddington. He is a consultant neurologist in Exeter, and editor of the *Journal of Medical Biography*. His train was late, and I sat around in the lounge for half an hour, watching businessmen exchange cards and tap on their laptops.

At last he arrived, and the meeting proved worth waiting for. Not only is Christopher Gardner-Thorpe a delightful man, with the typical St Philip's lack of arrogance, but he gave me two unforgettable vignettes. One was of the way Mr Tibbits ate his baked tomato.

The fact that he even had a baked tomato is worth noting. 'Mr Tibbits would have something quite different from us for lunch,' Christopher Gardner-Thorpe said. 'Quite often it was chops. Selected pupils were allowed to sit next to him, and I was quite often chosen.'

'Was it scary to sit next to him?'

'No, not scary at all. It was a pleasure. He was a good man, a kind man. He always liked to have a baked tomato, and he would put the flat of his knife on top of it and press down. It would go "splooch" everywhere. In fact, now I come to think of it, it was two baked tomatoes: a double-whammy.'

The other vignette was the beating one. 'If a boy knocked on the classroom door and said, "Mr Tibbits wants to see you", you knew what you were in for. He took you through his study into his bedroom and you had to kneel on a wooden stool and put your elbows on the bed. He had red and black slippers on a rack and would choose one. Your bare bottom was facing him. You got two, three or four whacks. I'd usually cry. Afterwards he'd put his arm round you and say, 'You won't do that again, will you?'

The twenty-first-century reader sees a whole Social Services' dossier of unsuitable behaviour in those words. Many St Philip's boys have described to me what it was like to be beaten by Mr Tibbits: it's one of the two things they remember most clearly, along with their least favourite school lunch. But every single boy has reiterated to me that Mr Tibbits's beating was not sadistic or sexual. 'It sounds awfully kinky now,' Christopher Gardner-Thorpe said to me. 'But I really don't think it was.'

The use of the marital bed as bend-over station seems to have stopped in the early 1950s. From then on it was the armchair in the headmaster's study.

'Tibbits was an overgrown schoolboy himself, really.' This was Christopher Gardner-Thorpe's mother's view. I went all the way to the Hop Barn Café in Uckfield, East Sussex, to meet Lady Hazel Gardner-Thorpe, who at 93 may well be the oldest St Philip's mother alive. She told me she had won the Mothers' Race on Sports Day in 1949. Now she is nifty with the Zimmer frame, and is happily settled at a nursing home run by Benedictine nuns. She remembers the Tibbitses as being '*very* nice' and that they once came to drinks in Pont Street. I asked her how she'd discovered the school. 'Oh, I enquired at the Oratory. We were *very* pleased to find a good Catholic school in the neighbourhood.'

Before taking the train to Uckfield, I met Julian Fellowes at a café in Sloane Square. Again, here was a highly successful man, an Oscar-winning scriptwriter, who had answered my e-mail to him within minutes and found a free hour within a fortnight. 'I came to St Philip's in 1955,' he told me. 'Two of my elder brothers,

David and Rory, went there too. We lived two doors away, at 2 Wetherby Place, which meant we were always late. Every day. It's impossible *not* to be late if you live as close as that to a school. Mr Tibbits got more and more exasperated, until eventually all three Fellowes boys were bent over and beaten for our lateness.'

Before going to St Philip's he had been at 'Russell's' (the 'Tibbits'-style nickname for Wetherby School) across the road; and after leaving at 11 he went to Gilling, the prep-school for Ampleforth. When I asked him whether Mr Tibbits was a frightening headmaster, he said,

I don't remember him with any rancour. At Gilling, I was put into the hands of a truly horrible headmaster, Father Hilary Barton, and I don't care who prints it. Father Barton was needlessly cruel, a hideous bully, and it's a mark of shame on the Benedictines that they allowed such a man to be a headmaster of young boys. I find as I get older that I forgive him less, not more. Beside him, Mr Tibbits was hardly terrifying at all. When you're young, the concept of absolute monarchy is less affronting than it is when you grow up. The fact that he was a person of all power was not particularly offensive. He wasn't a cosy man in any way – not "an uncle to all the boys" or anything like that.

And what about Mrs Tibbits? 'Well sometimes you might expect the wife of someone like that to offset her husband. But she was just as strict as he was.'

What did he make of the Tibbits marriage?

'In those days, headmasters had to be married. They were expected to demonstrate a blameless personal life. A bit like the Royal Family. I don't think it was any different for a landowner or an ambassador in those days. You had to be married, and married without problems.'

(This suggests that Mr Tibbits's decision to procure a wife for himself was a matter of the head rather than the heart. But we shall never know the truth about this.)

There were bombsites all around. 'My brother and I used to go off and explore them after school,' Julian Fellowes told me. 'We'd pick around in those ruined rooms. In the bombsite on Harrington Road we found a bust of William Pitt, and a silver clock which we had to hand in to the police. One day we went into a ruined lift and pressed the button. We were suddenly absolutely terrified that it would start going up and we'd be trapped.'

Fellowes remembers the moment when his lifelong fascination with history started. It was in the Big Schoolroom, one weekday morning.

There were always posters in there, hanging on clips. One morning I walked in and saw a picture of a beautiful woman in a dark dress, kneeling before the block. Behind her was a masked headsman holding his axe in the air, ready to strike. I asked the master, 'What's that?' 'That's Mary Queen of Scots,' he told me. I said, 'But if she was a Queen, why is she being executed?' 'Well, she was executed by her cousin who was Queen of England.'

I had the sudden feeling that the world was a much stranger place than I'd previously anticipated. That evening I went to the local library with my aunt and we found a biography of Mary Stuart . . .

'This was before Antonia Fraser had written hers,' I butted in, keen to name-drop another St Philip's mother.

'Oh, yes, *long* before Antonia wrote hers,' he replied, 'and there was a photograph of Mary Queen of Scots's death mask in it. From that stemmed my whole interest in history, which has informed a lot of my work. It all started in that room at St Philip's.'

*

Boys' prep schools have always attracted eccentric teachers. Young, dishevelled men who leave university without having a clue what to do next; fresh-faced railway-map enthusiasts unsuited to a job in the City; retired Army officers with very white legs who wear shorts in winter; blue-stocking women in a vain search for a husband; Catholic converts with a Third in History from Oxford, and so on. 'Read Waugh's *Decline and Fall*, and you have St Philip's in the 1940s and 50s,' more than one old boy has said to me.

Mrs Tibbits's descriptions of some of the early post-war St Philip's teachers bear this out. In the taped interview with Harry Biggs-Davison, she describes an extraordinary bunch of characters.

Brigadier Picton: 'He was sweet. Retired gunner. He taught maths very well.'

Miss Rosalind Niep: 'She was a marvellous person, really, frightfully funny and just like Joyce Grenfell. She used to look after her father at Beckenham. I went to the father's funeral. And some bloody cat of a woman said to me, "Oh,

Mrs Tibbits, Rosalind teaches with you, doesn't she?" "Yes," I said, "she's a most excellent person." "Oh," she said. "Is she sober when she comes to school?" And I said, "I don't know what you're talking about. I've never seen Rosalind anything but perfectly sober." And I turned my back on her. But later I rang up Mrs Ingham, a great friend of hers, and said "Is there any truth in it?" "Well," she said, "you know, there is.'"

Mr W: 'He was a classical Oxford thing, got Firsts and things. Dick wrote to his tutor to find out about him, and he said he was a very peculiar case and it would be a good thing if he settled down for a term or two. Unfortunately he boozed, we all knew that, but he managed to slope in here in the morning. He fell out of the window and broke his leg and arm and everything. You've no idea what we went through.'

Mr Pollard-Britton. 'He got the most awful passion for Felicity who was our school secretary. A perfect nuisance: he was always bringing her flowers, always chasing her around.'

Mr Jones: 'He was marvellous. A very clever young man. He had polio in one leg, yet he played cricket like fury with the boys, first game.'

Mr Neville: 'He appeared in a businessman's

suit every day. It was the exams and it was the hottest part of the year: boiling. Well, suddenly there was the most awful haroosh upstairs, Dick shouting, "Where are the examination papers, Neville?" There was Neville running up and downstairs like a madman: he couldn't find the papers. I've never seen a person in such a state. The coat came off and then the waistcoat came off this businessman's suit. Someone found the papers, but it was all too much for Neville. He left, and ran a launderette. Most peculiar. He was an Ampleforth chap.'

Mr Donellan: 'My pet aversion. He taught well. He came straight from Ealing.'

(What did Mrs Tibbits mean by 'straight from Ealing'? Did she mean 'he was straight out of an Ealing Comedy' or that he simply came directly along the District Line? What she did mean, I later found out and would never have guessed, was that he came straight from St Benedict's School, Ealing. And, though a 'pet aversion' of Mrs Tibbits, he was later to become an acclaimed theatre director.)

Mr Lavender: 'Frightfully nice. Really good, I think, at maths. He said to me once – he had a very Cockney way of talking – "I could buy the whole lot of you out." And he could. He was rolling. Really, the money was his wife's. He was one of these swimming experts; he used to go and judge the Olympics, and Mrs, too. They were an interesting couple. He'd been a customs officer abroad, and he retired, you see, and was good at maths, so he applied for a job here. It was extraordinary, Brigadier Picton all very posh and Army, and old Lavender: the contrast was incredible.'

Mr V.: 'Very unsatisfactory. I think he was too idle to teach. A nasty bit of work. He did a very dirty trick to an Irish boy we had. At the games field this Irish boy found a five-pound note on the ground. He picked it up and said "Sir, I've found a five-pound note," and V. said, "Give it to me. I'm going to have that," and he put it in his pocket. Well, the next day the boy came and told Dick. Then there was an awful haroosh. [Clearly a favourite Mrs Tibbits word.] V. was always short of money. He married a barmaid in Esher who was pregnant by another man.'

And lastly, the French teacher Mr Tregear. All the 1950s and 1960s old boys I spoke to remembered Mr Tregear. And all of them, quite separately, said similar things. Rocco Forte: 'Very concerned about his

Sacré
bleu!

appearance.' Marius Barran: 'One didn't judge people at our age, but in retrospect he made Kenneth Williams look like a truck-driver.' Julian Barran: 'He was a real dandy. He wore black boots with red cork high heels and drainpipe trousers with a double seam.' Peter Landau: 'I remember this man who taught us French. He wore this obvious toupé like an old rat on his head. He liked to wear low-waisted trousers and four-inch-wide leather belts.'

These remarks show how dazzling coloured clothes were at a time when most teachers wore brown corduroy and tweed.

As for Mrs Tibbits's memories of Mr Tregear, there were two dark episodes. The first was when he feigned a heart attack on the day the school inspectors came. (This episode really is 'straight from Ealing'.)

John Tregear didn't want the inspector Miss Berwick (who was an absolute tartar) to take his French class. So he suddenly had a heart attack. He screamed and shouted, 'Ooh, I'm so ill, so ill.' I felt inclined to hit him because I knew he was pretending. Dick said we'd better call for an ambulance. The ambulance duly came and the one who had to go with him to hospital was me. He shouted and screamed in the ambulance, 'I want a private room, Mrs Tibbits!' And, 'Get me a priest!' I felt inclined to say, 'Well you're one yourself: get on with it.' He had been ordained, though no one knew it when he was here. He was in hospital for three weeks, though I swear there was nothing wrong with him.

And what did the school inspectors make of all this? 'Well, the first thing Miss Berwick said was, "I'll go and take Mr Tregear's French class." So you see he hadn't achieved anything with his heart attack.'

The second episode was extremely short and marked the end of Mr Tregear's career at St Philip's. He had always boasted that one day when his father died he was going to inherit a fortune, and then he wouldn't need to be a teacher any more. 'He rang up at eight on a weekday morning [said Mrs Tibbits] and said, "My father's dead. I'm not coming back." We never saw him again.'

And that was it. As Harry Biggs-Davison put it to me simply: 'He buggered off.'

*

From this ragbag of untrained teachers came some erratic but occasionally inspired teaching, unhampered by any National Curriculum.

'Which of you boys can read?'

Marius Barran remembers being asked this by the form teacher, Mr Thompson, on his first day at the school in 1954.

'Three of us put our hands up – I and Adam Zamoyski and Michael Lieven, all of whom are still my friends,' he told me. 'I'm an architect, Adam's a historian and Michael's an academic. Mr Thompson said, "Right. You three can take books off the shelves and read them. Meanwhile I'll teach the rest of the class to read." We each picked a book off the shelf. I chose *David Copperfield*, which was a bit difficult as I was only 7. Michael suggested *Poo Lorn of the Elephants* by Reginald Campbell, which was much more suitable.'

The three boys just sat and read their books for a few days until the rest of the class reached a decent standard of literacy.

Presiding over the whole scene was Mr Tibbits himself, who (as Antonia Fraser's brother Michael Pakenham told me) was 'a bloody good headmaster. I came aged 6 from a village school in Sussex so I wasn't the finished article. I wasn't even the begun article. I started learning Latin and became strong very quickly. You did your homework every night: you didn't muck about. Tibbits really cared about academic achievement. I remember that on the day I got a scholarship to Ampleforth he declared a half-holiday for the school. The message was: 'Do well at your books, boys, and you'll be popular.'

'Tibbits was a driving force,' Michael Pakenham's brother Kevin told me. 'He had this whole view of bringing up boys in old-fashioned ways; making them into young Catholic gentlemen. He had an enormous temper. He could go from sunshine to thunder in seconds. But he was tremendously charismatic. His wife was always known as "Moon". I'm not quite sure why. Perhaps it was because she was the moon to his sun.'

3

Austerity and Boys' Mince

We've been trained, by books and television programmes on 'Austerity Britain', to think of the late 1940s and early 1950s as brownish-grey years when everyone was cold and, if not actually hungry, then full up on the nastiest kind of cheap stodge.

I tried to draw St Philip's old boys out on this, asking them questions like, 'Did you feel you were living in an age of austerity?' and 'Do you remember the winter of 1947?' Oddly enough, most of them could not be drawn out on this. Prep-school boys didn't notice such things, it seems. You didn't expect school food to be anything other than foul, or games fields in winter to be anything other than frozen wastes.

The most cinematic depiction of 1950s London was given to me by David Stockley, who lived in The Boltons and walked home after school in such thick pea-souper fogs that he had to feel his way by clutching the railings. He remembered the dim yellow lights of cars as he cautiously crossed the Old Brompton Road.

Boys walked to and from school from the age of 8. 'Everyone thought it was perfectly natural,' Michael Pakenham told me. 'My parents lived in Cheyne Gardens – I remember that my father [Lord (Frank) Pakenham] had just become Chairman of the National Bank, earning £5,000 a year – and for four years I did that walk by myself every day. It took half an hour.' 'I walked to school across Onslow Gardens,' Simon Hunt said. 'It was bare earth, as it had been requisitioned.' 'On the way home after games we used to sneak into the Odeon Kensington without paying, through the "push-bars",' Peter Landau told me. 'You can imagine it: four or five small boys in uniform, trying not to be noticed in the back row.'

Only the boys in the top two years wore long trousers: the rest wore shorts. Thinking of these bare-kneed boys walking the streets of London unsupervised, sneaking into the cinema after games, taking buses and tube trains, playing on the bombsites, it's impossible not to be nostalgic for this lost era of freedom. But there were other ways in which St Philip's boys were less free than they are now. For example, they had to eat everything on their plate.

*

Unless, that is, they went home for lunch. 'I never once had lunch at school,' Peter Landau said. 'My grand-mother and my maiden aunt were at home, so there was always someone there. On games days I went directly from home to the games field in Barnes.'

Why didn't more boys elect to have lunch at home? I would have travelled to the end of the Central Line and back to avoid some of the more appalling food-stuffs that the boys (but not their headmaster) were forced to eat. Years later, Harry Biggs-Davison discov-ered, at the bottom of a drawer of Mr Tibbits's desk, an old invoice from the local butcher: 'Four rump steaks; 5 lbs of boys' mince.'

Making their sons stay to lunch was, I suppose, the other side of the same coin of parental lack of involve-ment. The very parents who didn't worry if their boys were an hour late home from school were quite happy to hand them over to enforced consumption of what-ever horrors lurked in 'boys' mince'.

For Michael Rappazini (who started at the school when it re-opened in 1947), it was the lumpy custard that he loathed. 'To this day, I can't eat *crème anglaise*.' His parents ran a restaurant, the Maison Basque in Dover Street, so he was particularly sensitive to good and bad cooking. 'If you wanted to avoid afternoon lessons, you didn't finish your lunch, as you were made to sit in front of it till you had eaten every mouthful. I remember the grey, watery mashed potatoes with not a trace of milk or butter.'

For Michael Pakenham, it was Heinz spaghetti in tomato sauce with onions in it. 'It's the only true horror story of the first ten years of my life,' he said. 'I was just unable to eat it. It quickly went cold, of course. I remember the coagulated cold spaghetti looking at me from the plate. If you didn't finish, the whole school had to sit there and wait until you had. I tried various stratagems, such as loading it into a handkerchief and putting it in my trouser pocket, but none of them worked. I still hate onions.'

'I didn't like the puddings,' Edward Coventry said. 'It was often a blancmange-type thing with a very thick skin. One noticed a thin layer of dust on top. I remember sitting next to a boy who was having trouble eating his blancmange. The whole school was waiting. He was taking tiny little mouthfuls. Then suddenly he leaped up from the table to vomit in the garden. I asked him what had made him leap up like that. He said, "I suddenly encountered a cabbage leaf."'

'The food was particularly disgusting on Friday,' Kevin Pakenham told me. 'I still can't eat cod. It was in batter with a thin tomato sauce. If I didn't throw up with the fish, I did with the blancmange we were given for pudding.'

Julian Barran remembers differently. 'The food was excellent,' he said. 'I loved the banana custard. Also the stews with carrots in them.' His memories of the school are unclouded by any kind of trauma. 'I came away with absolutely no scars or feelings of resentment, and one really got a good education.'

*

As for the beatings, Julian Barran said, 'Oh yes, Tibbits used to beat one if one was naughty. But he was a very nice, decent man and he genuinely cared about children.'

It was fairly common for middle-aged men to emerge from their military war years more irascible than they had been before the war. Whether Mr Tibbits's irascibility was caused by serving in the Army under the 'loathsome' George Wigg; or by some appalling and shocking wartime experience; or by general mid-life grumpiness; or by dyspepsia; or (heaven forbid) by living cooped up in a small flat on top of the school with Mrs Tibbits, we do not know. But all the post-war St Philip's boys I have spoken to have told me of his sudden changes of mood. Gerard Noel had no recollection at all of this irascibility – or of any corporal punishment – in the pre-war years.

'If you got less than six out of ten in the Monday morning Latin test,' Simon Hunt told me, 'you got the slipper. It hurt; it stung. But I didn't feel any rancour about it.' 'It did hurt quite a lot,' David Stockley said. 'It was a nuisance that it was so painful. That being said, it was quick. Much shorter than detention. Ten minutes later, you didn't notice it at all.' He and Adam Zamoyski remember being beaten for 'making faces' and 'fooling around' rather than for doing badly in tests.

'"Slipper" was a misnomer,' Kevin Pakenham told me. 'It was a shoe. And not a soft shoe, either: one with a heel. (Other boys have told me it was definitely a worn-out old slipper. Clearly there was a range of footwear.) And it was Kevin Pakenham who told me about the red light.

'A red light?'

'Yes, he used to switch on a red light outside his study door, which meant that someone was being beaten.'

It must have happened one day, then, that Mr Tibbits employed an electrician to install a light outside his study, and he must have stipulated that the light bulb be red; and Mrs Tibbits (who was in charge of keeping house) must have kept a stock of red light bulbs for this particular light fitting. It was a cunning strategy for instilling fear in the boys; and it certainly made them learn their Latin verbs.

Mr Tibbits also seems to have seen it as his own duty to explain the facts of life to the boys in the top year. Christopher Gardner-Thorpe remembers being taken aside just before he left the school, and asked by Mr Tibbits, 'Do you know the role your father played?' No actual anatomical parts were named in these talks. Ronald de la Grange, leaving the school in 1952, remembers 'a conversation so vague that I didn't realize what Mr Tibbits was talking about'.

*

It was in 1952 that Mrs Tibbits's nephew David Atkinson came to the school as a junior master. He left to do military service for two years, partly in Kenya, where he developed a passion for butterfly-collecting. He returned in 1954, from which time he stayed until his retirement in 1998. On his return from the RAF in 1954, he was the instigator of physical jerks.

'I remember doing the most dreadful PT in the garden,' Julian Barran told me. 'One had to stand in long lines, throwing one's chest out.' 'We did drill once a day at break-time,' Edward Coventry said. 'All in lines,

the left hand touching the right toe, and so on.'

The idea was to give a hundred boys a quick dose of exercise before getting back to lessons. Army life had rubbed off on Tibbits to such an extent that the military aura of the school was pronounced. The houses were called 'squads' and the house captains were 'squad commanders'. The squads were not (as the houses charmingly are now) named after Catholic saints. They were (unromantically) identified by colour: Red, Blue, Yellow, Green, Purple and Brown.

More vigorous exercise took place twice a week on the games field, which from 1947 onwards was 'the Harrods ground' in Lonsdale Road, Barnes – now the grounds of the Harrodian School. The rota was set in stone: football in the Michaelmas term, rugby in the Lent term, cricket in the summer term. Mr Tibbits was passionate about games. You didn't have much chance of being a 'squad commander' if you weren't good at them.

'The wind used to blow across that playing field like the winds of Siberia,' Edward Coventry said. 'Regardless of the cold, you had to wear just shorts and a shirt. That was the rule.' Underpants were forbidden during games, and the shorts were made of itchy wool. Boys remember Mr Tibbits standing by the pavilion banging his walking-stick on the ground with frustration during matches. 'The boy's useless!'

'Sports are my happiest memories,' Michael Pakenham said. 'Lovely grounds, terrific pitches, good pavilion.' 'I was good at games and was in the football, rugby and cricket First XI,' said Rocco Forte. 'We played ten matches each term against other schools.' The rewards for doing well and pleasing the head-master were high. Many old boys I have met showed me the miniature cups they were given as prizes. 'I won seventeen of them,' Peter Landau proudly told me, 'and I've kept them all my life.'

The walking-stick begins to be mentioned in the 1950s: Mr Tibbits seems to have acquired a limp during the war. This affected his driving. His foot would flop off the clutch when he was changing gear. Adam Zamoyski remembers him driving carloads of boys to and from the games field in 'this great big Humber Snipe with rust holes in the doors. He'd peer over the bonnet and curse other drivers. "Blithering idiot! Blithering idiot!"'

The other major Tibbits-walking-stick memory for boys is the swimming-pool one. In the humid and chlorine-heavy atmosphere of the Chelsea Baths, the fully dressed and overweight headmaster would stand clutching the pillars, oozing sweat and short of breath. If a boy was having trouble completing his length, Mr

Tibbits would hold his walking-stick out over the pool as a lifeline. 'I was terrified [remembers Marius Barran] that I was going to pull this great fat man in.'

I heard a great deal about swimming at the Chelsea Baths: the weekly visits, the 'plunging race', in which the strong swimmers would dive in at the deep end and see how far they could go without doing a single stroke. Mr Tibbits was the judge of this competition. He would walk along, stop where the boy stopped, and pace out the distance.

But Edward Coventry alerted me to a startling fact: 80 per cent of the boys couldn't swim, and never learned to during their whole time at St Philip's. 'There was a great deal of jumping up and down and splashing, but we were never actually taught to swim. Mr Tibbits invented the "walking race" for the non-swimmers. We just waddled back and forth in the shallow end.'

It took the saintly Miss Cramer, in her pink swimming-cap which made her look bald, to change this. But that happened later.

The other hearty school activity was boxing. It was a compulsory part of school life. According to Roger Taylor, who was at Downside as a schoolboy, St Philip's was renowned as 'the boxing school'. The old St Philip's boys I have spoken to have vivid memories of skinny little boys in huge boxing gloves. On one afternoon each week the Big Schoolroom was converted into a boxing-ring with ropes round the edge.

The twenty-first-century mother is shocked by this active promotion of a punching sport. But boys do not seem to have been traumatized by it. Some (such as Rocco Forte) loved it. 'I was Captain,' he told me. 'We had boxing classes once a week and an annual tournament.' Boys who hated the icy games field liked boxing because at least you kept warm. 'We were really *taught* how to do it,' said Edward Coventry. 'We had a mixed-race master, an Afro-European, who was an excellent teacher. He used to get down on his hands and knees and demonstrate. The parents were invited to the annual tournament in one of the rooms at the Oratory, and it was there that I won this little cup.' 'Boxing certainly taught you not to be frightened of being hit,' said David Stockley.

There was a little Italian boy called Galli who was a particularly fierce and brilliant boxer. Lots of 1950s old boys remember him.

*

The surname 'Galli' prompts us to ask: how international was the 1950s clientèle? Were the surnames of St Philip's boys (as they are now) a seductive mixture of exotic European and English recusant, with the occasional modest square English surname thrown in (converts, Anglicans, etc)?

It seems as if the answer is yes. The exotic mix started after the war. In 1936 the surnames were all British/Irish: Noel, Edwards, Benton Rowell, Eaton, Pollen, Coates, O'Gorman, Hillier, Lowndes, Harvey, Newell, Bertie, McIntyre.

By the 1950s, foreign diplomats' and ambassadors' sons had started going to the school. Old boys remember Lauro Muller's birthday parties at the Brazilian Embassy (his father was First Secretary), with its huge spiral staircase whose long banister could be used as a slide. It was at one of these parties that Edward Coventry first discovered the attractions of 'these got-up and brushed-up and polished-up Latin-American girls. I remember thinking, "If I ever get married it's going to be to a Latin-American girl." By a twist of fate, that's exactly what happened.'

Among other names were: Rocco Forte and his cousin Juliano; Dominic and Tony de Souza-Pernes; Henry Togna and Michael and Richard Rappazini, whose parents were in the Italian restaurant trade; Gonzales Calderon, the son of the Spanish Consul; Polish boys such as Jan Chudzynski, Adam Zamoyski and a boy with the surname Ćwikła (the Tibbitses always pronounced it 'Quickler' – no effort was made to say it in a Polish way); Philip Peck from Doncaster, whose father was a conjuror; Nicholas Carr-Saunders, who became a pioneer of the wholefood movement and started Neal's Yard; Edmund Grey, whose father was Curator of Oriental Antiquities at the British Museum; Julian, David and Rory Fellowes, whose grandmother had converted to Catholicism along with their 12-year-old father ('we were the first *cradle-*Catholics in our family,' Julian Fellowes told me); the Pakenham boys, whose Fraser nephews and great-nephews would follow them to the school; Michael Lieven, the son of a Russian émigré prince; Julian Raby, a Baghdadi Jew's son, now the Director of the Freer and Seckler Galleries at the Smithsonian Institution in Washington; Mark Girouard who became the well-known architectural writer; and Matthew and Louis Jebb, sons of the architect Philip Jebb.

What was it like to be a Polish boy on your first day at the school? Adam Zamoyski remembers it vividly. He was one of the three boys who knew how to read, in Marius Barran's recollections above. Here he told me of a second unforgettable incident on that first day.

I joined in mid-year, in 1956. We had a history les-son in the back room with Mr Atkinson. He said,

'Now, I've got some administrative things to get on with, so why don't you all get on and draw a picture? What would you like to draw a picture of?' Overwhelmingly they voted for 'The Battle of Britain'. Having only recently arrived in London I'd never heard of this battle. I'd heard of lots of battles of towns and cities but I'd never heard of a battle of a country. 'Please, sir,' I asked, 'What's the Battle of Britain?'

It was a terrible moment. The whole class stared at me in astonishment – and hostile astonishment. It was as if a Communist Jew had walked into a Nazi Party rally. 'What's your name?' Mr Atkinson asked me. 'Adam Zamoyski, sir,' I said. 'Well,' he said, 'you should know, because if it hadn't been for the Poles we might not have won it.'

Zamoyski is eternally grateful to Mr Atkinson for having defused the situation so decisively and considerately. From that moment there was a bond between them. Mr Atkinson had an instinctive compassion for the underdog. He liked the idea of 'Gallant little Poland fighting on'. He soon spotted Zamoyski's genuine interest in history, and started taking him mudlarking on the Thames (one of his favourite hobbies) on Saturdays, in search of clay tobacco pipes, bits of pottery and old coins.

Adam Zamoyski gives us one of the earliest glimpses of Mr Atkinson as inspirer of future historians. 'He was really an overgrown boy scout. He had lots of little boyish enthusiasms, which he passed on to me. He opened my eyes to all sorts of things. You know those people who take you for walks in the country and can differentiate all the varieties of trees and moss and birds' eggs? Well, Mr Atkinson was the urban equivalent.'

As they walked the streets of London towards Queenhithe in the City (the prime mudlarking spot), Mr Atkinson alerted Zamoyski to the following urban details:

Coal-hole covers. 'Mr Atkinson said we should look at them. Each one had the maker's name, and different designs, and patent locks. I don't know if he ever took any rubbings.'

Standing bollards. 'He explained to me that bollards were originally cannons captured in the Napoleonic Wars. They had a cannon ball in the top. For ever after, bollards have been based on cannons.'

Fanlights. 'He told me how you could tell the different periods of the houses from the pattern.'

York stone paving. 'He told me that York stone paving-stones used to be turned over when they got old and worn.'

This was before they even got to Queenhithe. Then the real fun started, as they rummaged in the mud for items of historical interest. David Atkinson was a passionate enthusiast about clay tobacco pipes, to such an extent that he was later to be elected a Fellow of the Society of Antiquaries in recognition of his advances in the sum of clay-pipes knowledge. He wrote learned papers entitled 'Tobacco Pipes of Broseley, Shropshire', 'Sussex Clay Tobacco Pipes and the Pipemakers', and 'Makers' Marks on London Clay Tobacco Pipes'. Over his fifty-five years at St Philip's he tried (sometimes successfully) to instil this enthusiasm in the more historically impressionable pupils.

'Prep school sets you on the course of the rest of your life,' Edward Coventry said to me. It does seem that it is often in those years between 8 and 13 that a tiny spark is lit by a teacher telling you or showing you something, and that if you're lucky, that spark keeps alight and gradually becomes the glowing fire of your lifelong passion and career. That is certainly what happened to Adam Zamoyski, who grew up to be a historian of Polish events and people.

It happened also to Julian Fellowes's elder brother Rory, who came to the school in 1952, aged 6. He now runs Rory Fellowes Animations, travelling all over Europe and Scandinavia to make films. His lifelong passions for travel and art were ignited at St Philip's, and he remembers the very lessons that sparked them.

The passion for travel was started thus:

We were reading about Lapland. We learned a truly disgusting fact. A Lapp family would have one big bowl of water. The father would wash in it, and spit into it and blow his nose, and then it would be passed to the mother, who'd do the same, and then it would be passed on down the family, getting more and more revolting until the youngest child got it. It was such a vivid picture: this family sitting in a circle in the deep snow, passing the bowl round. It started my curiosity about foreign lives, and it made a traveller out of me.

And the passion for art: 'We had to trace Highland cattle. My grandmother was a Macintosh so I did have some Scottish blood, and I drew a good picture: actually, for me it was a triumph. It really looked like a Highland cow. I kept it for years; and from that moment on, I wanted to be an artist.'

I suppose you can't give all the credit to a teacher for

inspiring someone's whole, lifelong interest. The passion would probably have flared in some other way, if it hadn't happened at that specific moment. But these vivid recollections of the moment of combustion are nonetheless touching. As Adam Zamoyski said to me, 'Ninety per cent of the teachers at St Philip's – as well as at Ampleforth where I went later – were certifiable. They wouldn't be allowed within a mile of a school now. But that was often what made them such good teachers.'

'By the age of 7 I was reading *Treasure Island*,' Rory Fellowes told me. 'You were *expected* to be good at drawing, good at reading, interested in foreign lands.'

This atmosphere of high expectation was nurtured by the ever-present R. H. Tibbits. His care for the intellectual lives of his pupils was matched only by his care for their spiritual lives. He nourished them on a diet of high achievement and High Catholicism. All the 1950s old boys I have spoken to remember the walks in crocodiles to the Oratory for Mass and confession three or four times a term. The Oratory was integral to the school, having been behind its very founding in 1934, and having inspired its name.

But when, two-thirds of the way through the next decade, Mr Tibbits was to die of a sudden heart attack, the Oratory would sever its relations with St Philip's for twenty-three years.

4

A Deathbed Scene

As we turn the corner into the 1960s, we say goodbye to the Ancient Historic era of St Philip's, and approach the Recent Historic era. Any historian of St Philip's develops a psychological calendar: not BC and AD, but BHBD and AHBD. The new era begins in September 1963 when a 7-year-old boy called Harry Biggs-Davison arrives at the school as a new boy. From that first nervous morning up until and including the present day, Harry Biggs-Davison's only term-time absences have been during his five-year spell at Downside and his three-year spell at Cambridge in the 1970s.

'Did you have any inkling, that first day when you were quaking at your desk, that you would one day be headmaster?' I asked him.

'None at all. Although from an early age I was interested in teaching. I came back as junior master in the year after leaving Downside, and I have to say, I loved it.'

'What do you remember about your first weeks at the school?'

'I remember being totally in awe of Mr Tibbits. He had the most tremendous temper. It didn't surface often, but when it did it was terrifying. I always looked forward to his RK lessons. He'd start with a round-the-class quiz. "What Sunday is it this week?" "What colour vestments will the priest wear?" and so on. There was a boy in our class called Mark Babington – quite a big bruiser of a boy – and when Mr Tibbits fired one of the quiz questions at him, he replied, "I haven't got the *faintest* idea." Tibbits exploded. Out came torrents of invective. He was slamming his stick on the desk.'

A 'but' almost always follows any description of the Tibbits loss of temper. 'But mostly,' said Harry Biggs-Davison, 'he was very compassionate and gentle – as long as you were polite. He knew his boys. His health was quite poor by the time I knew him. He'd lost a lung. He was ill a lot of the time, with a bad cough. He drank and smoked quite heavily and was overweight.'

We have paper proof about the smoking: an invoice survives from early 1963, showing that Mr Tibbits ordered 1,200 Players cigarettes a month.

In fact, now aged 60, he only had three and a half years to live. But he was to carry on being headmaster up until the last day of his life.

*

Two women had come quietly on to the St Philip's scene in the late 1950s: Miss Cramer and Mrs Tolmie. They were to teach at the school for the next three decades. Sometimes it's hard to tell legendary bluestocking female teachers apart. Too often, the blanket term 'battle-axe' is used to describe such ladies. It doesn't do justice to the saintliness beneath. Here are brief descriptions of each of them to show just how different they actually were. Remember, one was Miss and the other was Mrs.

First, Miss Cramer. Her Christian name was Priscilla. She was thin, and came and went each day on a bicycle. She wore black, and her hair was pinned up in a bun, except during swimming lessons when it was in a pink cap. She was the class teacher for the younger boys, strict but kind, and she had impeccable italic handwriting. She cared passionately about neat handwriting, correct spelling and faultless grammar. It was Miss Cramer who, at the Chelsea Baths, got the younger boys doggy-paddling and later swimming, thus bringing an end to the embarrassing tradition of scores of St Philip's boys waddling about in the shallow end, unable to swim a stroke.

Her brother was a monk at Ampleforth, Father

Anselm Cramer. Her nephew Peter Cramer is a don at Winchester College, and I visited him to try to find out the 'back story' of his aunt, whom so many ex-St Philip's boys thank for their legible handwriting in adulthood.

'We always knew her as "Aunt Cilla",' Peter Cramer said. 'She lived in Mount Street in Mayfair with her mother – my grandmother – whom she looked after, doing all the cooking and shopping.

'She was tireless. She did masses and masses of work for charity in her parish, St Mary's Cadogan Street. She was always doing things for other people. She became hunched from exertion. Occasionally she would get us nephews and nieces up to London, and take us to museums relentlessly for the whole day, and then to the theatre in the evening. I remember being so exhausted after a day of this that in the taxi home I was thinking, "Have I even got the energy to be polite any more?"'

Cramer remembers looking into his aunt's refrigerator and finding tiny, teaspoon-sized leftovers. Nothing was wasted in this little mother-and-daughter household. 'We always said, "What's going to happen to Aunt Cilla when our grandmother dies?" – never suspecting that she would be the first to die. She died of *old age* in her fifties. My grandmother found her dead in bed when she hadn't brought in the tea.'

That was years later, of course, in 1980. But this thumbnail sketch gives a vivid sense of the fullness and selflessness of Miss Cramer's short life. We must think of her working herself, day in, day out, towards an early grave.

Next, Mrs Tolmie. Her Christian name was Deirdre. She was short and stout, with a large nose – 'rather like Queen Victoria', according to her niece Harriot Rennie who is now the school secretary. Mrs Tolmie was far from being a childless spinster. The eldest of five children, from a large Catholic family, she had five daughters of her own. Her husband, the advertising manager for Johnnie Walker whisky, died in his fifties, and teaching at St Philip's gave Mrs Tolmie the focus that she craved in her later years.

Her mother had been running a boys' pre-prep school attached to the Maria Assumpta convent in Kensington at the time when Mr Tibbits had founded St Philip's in the 1930s, and had supplied him with some of his earliest pupils. Thus the connection between Mrs Tolmie's family and St Philip's spans the whole life of the school.

Whereas Miss Cramer's area of expertise was English, Mrs Tolmie's was Latin. She arrived at the school as secretary to Mr Tibbits, but quickly moved across to Latin teaching, and proved good at it. She gave boys the grounding in conjugations and declensions that prepared them for Common Entrance Latin at the top of the school. She also told Old Testament stories (Moses, the Ten Commandments) to the junior boys who sat on the floor at her feet. After lunch on Fridays she would take a train to her cottage in Somerset, with a rucksack on her back.

As she grew older her ankles swelled and she found the stairs at St Philip's increasingly hard. By the end she couldn't climb them at all, and had to have her classroom on the ground floor, where she would often fall asleep. It was the strange and peaceful sight of Mrs Tolmie fast asleep in her chair that greeted Anthony Jeffery when he arrived for his interview for the post of Head of English in 1989.

But now, in the early 1960s, she and Miss Cramer were young and sprightly. Their fellow members of staff included some of the eccentrics mentioned in Chapter 2 who had managed to stay on. The French teacher Mr Tregear had not yet inherited his fortune, and was still there, in his drainpipe trousers; and old pipe-smoking Mr Lavender, the Cockney millionaire, was still teaching maths – not particularly well, according to Nicholas May, who was a good mathematician and taught himself calculus at the age of 12. 'I thought I'd better keep that a secret from Mr Lavender.'

The teaching was old-fashioned, and sometimes downright out-of-date. Textbooks had not been renewed since the founding of the school: in geography lessons, 1960s boys found themselves learning about the exciting new invention of the mechanical combine harvester – which had actually come into widespread use in the 1930s. Miss Cramer, as well as teaching English, taught French to the younger boys, and Cyril Kinsky remembers her teaching them that the French for 'girl' was *une fillette* – a quaint old nineteenth-century word.

Mr Atkinson was never one for keeping up with the times. He spoke out vociferously against the switch to decimal currency. He didn't like things to be either newfangled or foreign. Louis Jebb remembers him asking, 'WHICH BOY has done this French "7" with a line through it?' Races at school sports days continued to be measured in yards for many years after most schools had gone metric.

But Atkinson was 'a darned good history master', as Harry Biggs-Davison remembers. He taught history from a huge file he'd made himself: Stone Age, Bronze Age, Iron Age, Romans, Saxons, Vikings, Normans, and so on. In their five-year spell at the school, boys would be taken through this simplified but vivid chronology, Mr Atkinson bringing each era to life with stories of heroes and villains, battles lost and won, underdogs beating overdogs, Great Britain winning against the foe. Major-General Sebastian Roberts, the eldest of the seven Roberts brothers who went to the school, thanks Mr Atkinson's history lessons for inspiring him to join the Army: 'His lessons attracted me to history, and my love of history attracted me to the military, without a shadow of doubt.'

Atkinson's patriotism can seem slightly xenophobic by twenty-first-century standards. Louis Jebb remembers him referring to an Italian boy as 'Spaghetti'. He also remembers another haunting episode.

> We were taken to a Test Match at Lord's between England and Australia. This was an enormous treat. Australia played brilliantly: they were untouchable. It was the team with Robert Massie and Dennis Lillee. We were made to leave halfway through the day because England were doing badly. It seemed a strange example to set to a group of 11-year-old boys.

Mr Atkinson's character matters, because he was soon to become the headmaster of the school and would remain in the post for over twenty years. The world is divided. To some, he was oddly jealous and prickly. To others, he was simply 'a lovely man'.

*

There were two annual school outings: one to London Zoo straight after pancakes on Shrove Tuesday; and one to Box Hill on Ascension Day, with water pistols. Most old boys I have spoken to can hardly remember the London Zoo outing, because the vividness of the Box Hill one has caused it to pale into insignificance.

'Hardly a picnic *à la* Jane Austen's *Emma,*' as one of them summed up the Box Hill day. Yes – certainly no elegant Regency manners or small talk. The moment the boys arrived they poured out of the coach and raced down the hill on foot or slid down on their bottoms to fill up their water-pistols from the stream. Then they raced back up the hill and squirted each other and the teachers (Tibbits and Atkinson, in plastic macs, included) till all were dripping. Then back down the hill again for a refill. 'The best day of the year, by far' is the general recollection. Everyone got caked in mud, all the normal rules were suspended for a day, and you had permission to make as much noise as you liked. It was a day of pure, raw boyhood.

'It was *un jour de fou,*' Benjie Fraser said. 'All that squirting water at the teachers: it was a levelling thing. It's why I'm a socialist.'

Sometimes boys got lost and didn't come back to the

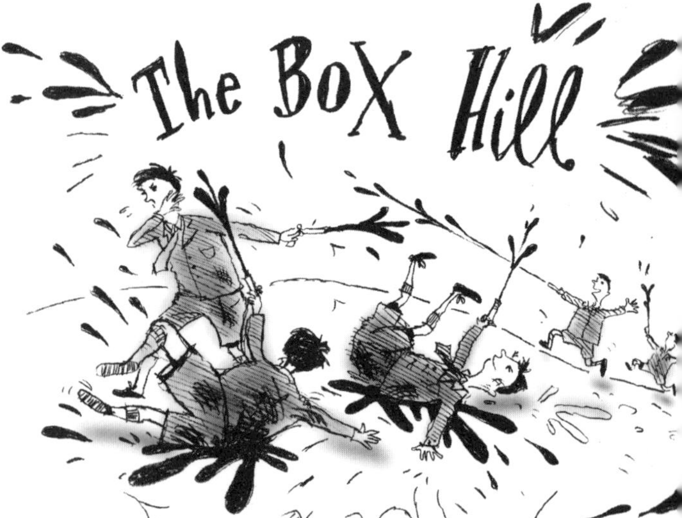
The Box Hill
Picnic

coach at the statutory hour of 4 p.m. Nowadays the reaction to this would be utter terror that the boy, or boys, had been injured or abducted. Then, it was simple annoyance. 'The wretched boy is *late*.' On one occasion Mr Atkinson had to stay behind for two hours, waiting for two vanished boys to return to the meeting-place.

*

Sweating, panting for breath, walking with a stick, Mr Tibbits was in gradual decline. He still liked a glass of sherry at lunch followed by red wine with his cheese course. His own menu remained different from that of the rest of the school. Nicholas May (the nephew of the 1950s non-swimming boy Edward Coventry, whom we met in Chapter 2) remembers another small but rankling injustice in the dining-room. It throws light on the importance of being good at sport at prep schools in those days.

'I was an academic type, not a sportsman. I was top of the form, and I was to go on to St Paul's. But because I wasn't sporty, I was not a Squad Commander or a "2nd". I was the only boy in the class not to be one of these. And if you were a Squad Commander or a "2nd", you got slightly bigger portion sizes at lunch – little extra things, the dumpling in the soup, for example – things I really found appetizing.' When I asked him whether the boys were still being beaten with a slipper in the 1960s (they were), he said, 'That didn't affect me nearly as much as feeling the poor relation at lunch.'

It was a harsh world. As a non-sporty boy, Nicholas May had to live with that daily injustice at the lunch table; but on the day of Mark Reading, it was the non-academic boys who suffered.

In the introduction to this history I hazarded guesses as to what 'Mark Reading' might mean. Gradually, talking to old boys, I found out. 'It was awful,' Harry Biggs-Davison told me. 'At the end of every term, every boy in the school had his marks read out and his position in the class announced in front of the whole school.' Boys were made to sit on the floor of the Big Schoolroom in formation, according to their form position. Mr Tibbits started at the top of the class, 'and the boys who were twentieth just sat there, waiting and waiting for their name to be read out'. No allowance was made for what is now known as dyslexia. Boys who had recently left the school were invited back as guests to watch this ritual humiliation of the stragglers.

John Shanahan, one of six Shanahan brothers who went to St Philip's (the others were Michael, Donal, Eamonn, Niall and Desmond) was definitely a Tibbits boy rather than an Atkinson boy.

'Atkinson didn't like me because at the age of 13 I was better than he was at football, and he hated that. He never made me captain of football, which I should have been. He never had anything to do with me. In fact, all of us Shanahans had problems with Atkinson. If we were beaten in a match against Aldro, we used to get such criticism from him!' (Aldro was where Mr Atkinson himself had been at school. He was particularly keen to win against it.)

John Shanahan and I were talking in the top-floor café of Peter Jones, in Sloane Square, but as I sat opposite him, listening to his stories of the triumphs and injustices of forty-six years ago, I could smell the grass and mud of 1960s pitches, and feel the raw emotion of winning and losing.

'Sport defined me,' he said. 'I was in the First XV for rugby for three years. We were unbeaten in 1964, we thrashed everyone who came in our way. Tom Biggs-Davison [the elder brother of Harry] was captain. In the cricket term I used to get up at 6 a.m. on match days – can you believe it? – and practise bowling against trees in the garden.'

Mr Tibbits adored John Shanahan, and John Shanahan revered his headmaster. 'He was a great figure in my life,' he told me. 'He was such a good *teacher*, apart from anything else. When he was telling us about the events of the first Easter morning, he made us think of the physical dead body of Jesus in the tomb. "Don't go in there, he stinketh!" He really brought the story to life.'

Both were passionate about sport. Both were the sons of GPs. 'D'you know, my father used to go out on his rounds in Warwick in a pony and trap,' Shanahan remembers Mr Tibbits telling him. Shanahan's description of what happened in 1965 gives an intimate glimpse of Mr Tibbits in his dying years.

> He started to get sick in the summer of 1965. He was in bed for a lot of that summer term, and he missed most of the matches. He lived in the flat two doors down from the school, and after every school cricket match I had to go into his flat and give him a complete run-down of the match.

Shanahan transported me mentally from the world of grassy pitches to the world of an old and ill man's bedroom.

> My father was a bit of an art collector, and on our wall at home we had an original etching of Rembrandt's *Death of the Virgin*. It was a dramatic death-bed scene – minions weeping all over the place, and the pallid dying Virgin in the middle.

Well, the sight of Mr Tibbits bedridden in 2 Wetherby Place reminded me strongly of this picture. His bedroom was full of Victoriana, cluttered and stuffy. There he lay, this big man, in his nightcap and nightshirt, propped up on the pillows, his limp hand dangling over the side of the bed. He used to take my hand – I remember being a bit embarrassed by this; I remember thinking, 'I'm blushing' – and prompt me for information about the match. He wanted to know the whole lot: every over. 'Tell me more, tell me more.' He'd been waiting all day for this. I used to see his face brighten as I recounted the matches; by the end he was a brighter spirit than the limp person he'd been when I came in.

These pre-mortem post-mortems brought incalculable cheer to Mr Tibbits's final two summers.

Mr Tibbits, it has to be said, was a particular friend of the Shanahan family; he used to go to dinner parties with John's parents, who lived near Lord's Cricket Ground and lent him a parking space for Test matches. 'Mr Tibbits made me feel pretty special,' John Shanahan told me. One might wonder whether this was mere favouritism, but I think this was not the case. There was a special empathy and affinity between the headmaster and this particular boy; but then Tibbits had the rare ability to make every boy in the school feel special and cared-about.

Here is a typical, random headmaster's report from *circa* 1957, a rare find among some old papers in Harry Biggs-Davison's possession. 'He has gone down several places. He does not worry at all and seeks only enjoyment. It is obvious by his report that he can do well in subjects he likes, so I will personally see to it that he applies himself to all equally. R. H. T.'

Every boy was under his watchful eye. He personally made sure that each one attained his best, both academically and spiritually.

*

Dom James Hood, now a chaplain at Downside, picks up the story where John Shanahan, at the bedside, left off. James Hood was on door duty as a school prefect on the fateful morning of Monday 8 May 1967. He arrived at 8 a.m., in blazer and tie, ready for a new school week in his Common Entrance term. There was an eerie silence about the place. Usually, Mrs Tibbits or Mr Atkinson had opened up the school by the time he arrived. But today, no one was there.

Fifteen minutes later, Mr Atkinson turned up, looking flustered. He opened up the school as normal. At assembly he made an announcement: 'I'm afraid Mr Tibbits is very ill. Let us pray for him.'

'We went off to our classrooms,' James Hood remembers. 'In the middle of the morning Mr Atkinson knocked on the door and asked our teacher to come out. We were left in the classroom, wondering what the reason might be. Then our teacher came back in and said, "There's going to be a late-morning assembly." So we all went back into the Big Schoolroom. Mr Atkinson came in, holding a missal. We knew something serious had happened. He told us that Mr Tibbits had died. We said prayers for him. We were told to go home, and we were each given a copy of a letter to take to our parents.

'I remember my mother saying, "Why are you back home so early?" I handed her the letter. Then I burst into tears.'

Some boys didn't manage to hold in the tears for so long: stifled sobs broke out round the room as soon as the news was announced. John Shanahan did manage to hold in the tears. 'I was at Worth by this time, and the news of Mr Tibbits's death was announced at Assembly, as there were quite a few ex-St Philip's boys here. I managed to hold it all in at assembly, but as soon as it was over I ran up to my bed and cried my eyes out.'

Mr Tibbits had died in his flat at 2 Wetherby Place. His death certificate named three causes of death: myocardial infarction, coronary ischemia and hypertension.

An end-of-Act-V-of-Shakespeare-tragedy feeling of emptiness and loss descended on the whole world of St Philip's and on everyone who had known him.

The letter each boy carried home to his parents informed them that the school would be closed for a week, and that Mr Atkinson would let them know as soon as possible whether it could carry on in the future.

*

The future was uncertain; but the present was busy. Preparations were made for a Requiem Mass at the Oratory. Mr Atkinson wrote out a timetable for the day, which survives in his elegant handwriting: '11.05 swimming as usual', and so on. '2.45: servers leave class and are taken to the Oratory by Mrs Tibbits.'

James Hood was one of the boys who went to the Oratory in 'Mrs Tibbits's limousine'. It was quite exciting, in its way. It was a white-shirt day. 'We were told not to wear a black tie, but our school tie,' Father Hood remembers, 'as that was what Mr Tibbits would have wanted.'

The Oratory was 'absolutely packed'. The Requiem Mass was beautiful; and there, behind the High Altar, was the painting of St Philip Neri, with his shield of three stars, its background the particular shade of blue that Mr Tibbits had chosen for the St Philip's blazer.

Mrs Tibbits left promptly after the Mass, James Hood remembers. Widowed for the second time, she was in no mood for chit-chat. Mr Atkinson stayed behind to talk to parents. He was now in charge. Both he and Mrs Tibbits were Anglicans. On the very evening of the Requiem Mass, he wrote this follow-up letter to parents:

You will naturally be anxious, following the sudden death of my Uncle, about your son's future education.

This is just to reassure you that the school will be carrying on as a Roman Catholic Preparatory School, as Mr Tibbits originally started it himself in 1934.

Having been here for fourteen years I am fortunately in the position of being able to carry on for Mrs Tibbits, which I intend to do to the best of my ability.

My Uncle taught me everything I know about schoolmastering and if I can achieve only a little of what he did I shall feel that I am not letting him down.

Please rest assured, too, that the religious side of the school has first priority and we have already taken steps to see that it will be maintained as all the parents will wish. The religious instruction will continue to be under the supervision of the Fathers of the Oratory.

I shall do my very best for each and every boy. Nothing will be too much trouble. Please do not hesitate to contact me if there is anything you would like to discuss.

Yours sincerely,
D. R. Atkinson

The balm of reassurance spread through the nervous systems of a hundred worried mothers. Atkinson's decency shone through in every sentence of this letter. The school would continue, and everything would (they hoped) be all right.

Letters of condolence and support poured in. One father had made a telling slip. 'Dear Mr Atkinson, Thank you for your letter about the future of St Tibbits.' He had scrubbed out 'Tibbits' and written 'Philip's' above it, with three exclamation marks. It showed how saintliness, school, Saint and headmaster were all intermingled in the public imagination.

*

Completely unaware of all these events, a young Oxford graduate applied for a job at the school in May 1967. The letter happened to land on the doormat on the very morning of Mr Tibbits's death. Mr Atkinson read it, and a fortnight later invited the young man to come for an interview.

This was Roger Taylor. With him, we sail into the late Sixties and on into the Seventies: the era when prep-school science teaching started. Mr Tibbits had always said, very firmly, 'Gentlemen do not study science.' After his death, this policy would change. It would still be many years before there was any kind of laboratory at the school. But there would, at least, be a Science Cupboard.

5

The Queen of the Staffroom

Mrs Tibbits's status changed overnight. She went from being wife of the headmaster to aunt of the head-master: quite a different thing.

This exchange of conversation was now frequently heard on the school stairs at 12.30.

Mrs Tibbits (in a piercingly loud voice, for she was going slightly deaf): 'DAVID! Are you com-ing to lunch? DAVID! It's lunchtime.'

David Atkinson (shuffling along the corridor in grey sleeveless V-neck, with his Jack Russell on a lead): 'Just walking the dog, Auntie!'

Mrs Tibbits: 'Tiresome boy!'

It can't have been easy for David Atkinson to assume the role of headmaster with his aunt keeping a watch-ful eye on him and calling him a tiresome boy. He did always dress like a schoolboy, and his whole outlook on life was that of a keen Boy Scout, so his aunt's way of talking to him is understandable. But it required a degree of long-suffering tolerance on his part to put up with it.

Mrs Tibbits certainly had no pretensions to being any kind of headmistress figure. Her role at the school had always been, and continued to be, purely domestic: overseeing the cooking and housekeeping, and sticking a plaster on to the occasional bleeding knee. But now, as aunt rather than wife of the headmaster, and as joint owner of the school with her nephew rather than her husband, she acquired more clout.

She became Queen of the Staffroom, in a more pronounced way than she had been during her late husband's lifetime. It was Mrs Tibbits, not her nephew the headmaster, who decided which members of staff were welcome to staffroom tea at the end of the day. As a rule, the female teachers (of whom there were never more than two) were given to understand that they weren't expected. They just quietly went home. When they'd gone, Mrs Tibbits would hand round a plate of triangular slices of white bread and butter to her chosen band of men; and then, when they'd eaten the bread and butter like good boys, she would cut the cake and give them a slice each. The scene is reminiscent of Margaret Thatcher surrounded by her all-male Cabinet.

She didn't like any interference from parents, especially mothers. If a mother rang the doorbell in the middle of the school day, because her son had forgotten his gym shoes, she would say, 'David! What's that woman doing here? What's she doing?'

Her nephew would explain the reason for the mother's brief visit.

His aunt would retort, 'The woman's mad! It's the Change of Life!'

She hadn't been nearly as raucous as this while her husband was still alive.

'Was Mr Atkinson quiet?' I asked Gavin Rankin, now the owner of Bellamy's restaurant in Mayfair, who was at St Philip's during the Tibbits-Atkinson handover. I had imagined (hearing from Denise Bolam the above descriptions of Mr Atkinson being affectionately submissive towards his aunt) that he might have been a fairly quiet chap all round.

'QUIET?' asked Gavin Rankin, astonished. 'He was one of the loudest people I ever came across. He could be very frightening if he wanted to. He was a stern disciplinarian: he had to be, I suppose – being in charge of a hundred little anarchists in a London townhouse.'

*

Mr Tibbits had inspired starry-eyed awe in his boys. It

was a hard act to follow. But in his solid, steady, stern way, Mr Atkinson kept the ship afloat. Thanks to his dislike of anything newfangled, hardly any changes were made. One small new tradition was introduced: that of playing 'Animal, vegetable, mineral' in the dining-room at the end of lunch, while waiting for the blancmange-detesters to struggle through their loathed bowlfuls.

'Nothing will be too much trouble,' he had written in that letter to parents after his uncle's death: and he remained as good as his word. Not only did he continue to teach history, vigorously, to all the boys in the top four years of the school, but in twenty-two years as headmaster he never missed an afternoon on the sports field. He turned out in all weathers, with his shorts on and his dog on a lead.

He had three Jack Russells in succession: 'Timmy-Tim-Timpots', 'Tommy-Tom-Tompots' and 'Sammy-Sam-Sampots'. If he stood up during a history lesson, to draw a wall-plan of the Battle of Agincourt, his dog would hop up on to his master's chair and appear to take charge.

Mr Atkinson never married. Denise Bolam, who arrived at the school as Miss McCartney in 1976 and is still there, only remembers one single time when he alluded to a possible Past. 'I was crying on the school doorstep one day,' she said, 'when I'd bust up with a boyfriend. David Atkinson came up to me, very concerned and sweet, and said, "I had a girlfriend once. I wouldn't bother about it again, if I were you."'

He was a man of simple needs and regular habits. He hated onions, and asked for them to be excluded from school catering. Best of all, he liked a boiled egg and toast. On Friday afternoons, his secretary gave him a Mars Bar to take with him on his drive down to the South Coast in his Morris Minor, where he spent the weekend with his mother.

He never shook off the competitive schoolboy's fierce desire to win matches. If St Philip's was beaten by a rival school, he was in a bad mood all the next day. 'You were treading on eggshells,' Harry Biggs-Davison recalls. 'I remember once,' Gavin Rankin said, 'he gave the whole First Eleven a black mark for being defeated. It was what you might call the Saddam Hussein approach to football management.'

Test cricket was high up in his life's priorities – especially if England was winning. 'When I came for my interview in 1968,' the Classics master John Milward told me, 'I asked David Atkinson, "D'you mind if we delay the interview to watch Colin Cowdray get his first century for England against Australia in England?" So we watched it on his television.' Their joint love of cricket gave them an instant bond. "'I think you'll be very happy here," David said to me – and it was very true.'

Mr Atkinson was something of a caner. Whereas with Mr Tibbits it had been pants down and slipper, with Mr Atkinson it was trousers on and cane. 'If you were sent out of class and found by him in the corridor, that meant only one thing,' Guy de Lotbinière remembers. 'Once, I was kicked out of the class by Mrs Lloyd-Webber [mother of Andrew and Julian, who taught singing at the school]. I ran up to the top of the house and hid till the bell went, so I avoided being caught and caned. That was my finest hour.'

Mr Atkinson was not raspingly rude about parents behind their backs, as Mrs Tibbits was. ('My PET HATE!' she used to say, of her least favourite ones.) But he didn't have much to do with them. He was there for the boys, not for the parents. Once, some parents had invited him to their house and given him fancy foreign food. So he never accepted an invitation from any parents again. He would only show one set of prospective parents round per week. He refused to show them round during the school day: it had to be in the late afternoon, when the school was deserted, so the visit was not atmospheric.

'Well, this is the school,' he would say, as he showed

parents into the empty classrooms. 'Jolly good school.' Marketing was not his forte.

All through his headmastership, he continued to take the historically minded boys mudlarking by the Thames on occasional Saturdays. Sometimes he took them further afield, out to the country overnight, to dig for clay pipes. Gavin Rankin recalled,

> I was the Victor Ludorum for swimming, and I liked history, so Mr Atkinson took me to Salisbury one weekend to dive for clay pipes in the river. We stayed at a coaching inn in Salisbury. He allowed me to have one glass of cider, I remember. It was beautiful by the river there, in those dappled meadows, with the cathedral spire above us. There was a lot of stuff in the river, Mr Atkinson said, and he wanted me to get it out. He pointed to a place and I dived in and came up with a great handful of clay-pipe fragments. You could see their makers' marks: it was fascinating. I've still got some of them in a box.

*

'The religious instruction will continue to be under the supervision of the Fathers of the Oratory,' Mr Atkinson had written in the letter to parents of May 1967: but this was one assurance he would not be able to abide by. Very soon after the death of Mr Tibbits, the Oratory severed its relations with St Philip's. Why was this?

The whole episode – and it is a long one, lasting twenty-three years – is rather vague now, and no one likes to talk about it. Mr Atkinson, writing in the second-ever issue of the *Three Stars* school magazine (July 1968), explained it thus: 'A change of parish boundaries not long ago resulted in our becoming part of the parish of the Carmelite Priory Church in Kensington.'

I've checked with the Diocese of Westminster, and have discovered that there was indeed a change of parish boundaries in 1967 – but the change was not away from the Oratory parish. It was from the parish of Our Lady of Victories to the newly created parish of the Carmelite Priory. Wetherby Place had never been in the Oratory parish at all. The connection between the Oratory and the school had been forged by the friendships of Mr Tibbits, the Oratory Fathers and the Catholic mothers who went to the Oratory on Sundays and were in need of a nearby prep school for their sons.

Relations with the Oratory were severed, in reality, partly because Mrs Tibbits and Mr Atkinson were Anglicans. Harry Biggs-Davison explained it to me in this way: 'We were never in the Oratory parish. In 1970 the Oratory School went Comprehensive and grew from 200 to over 1,000 pupils, and the Oratory's commitment to it grew. Tibbits had been a well-known and popular figure among the priests. As soon as he died, and there were two non-Catholics running St Philip's, it was the Oratory Fathers' excuse to be rid of their extra burden.'

And so St Philip's, cast adrift from the Oratory, turned north-westwards to the Carmelite Priory in Kensington Church Street for its spiritual guidance. Father Patrick Keely became the school chaplain – a softly spoken Irishman – 'from a different social background', as the French master Stephen de la Bedoyère tactfully put it to me. 'I loved the Carmelites,' said Benjie Fraser, who came to the school as a new boy in the late 1960s. 'They seemed more modest, more liberal, more live-and-let-live than the Oratory Fathers. I loved Father Keely.'

Mrs Tibbits could never quite hide her slight snobbishness towards people with Irish accents. When informed that a tramp had knocked on the door of the school begging for money, Mrs Tibbits said, loudly and within earshot of Father Keely, 'Was he IRISH?'

*

'Since records began.' This expression, most often used in the context of extremes of British weather, can also be used to describe the era at St Philip's from March 1968 onwards. For now the *Three Stars* came into existence. Edited by the English master Mr Irvine, typed on foolscap paper by the school secretary, stapled and stamped by the senior boys, it was published every term, so now we emerge into the blinding light of almost too much information.

All the names of the Squad Commanders and Squad Cup winners are listed in each issue. (So we can see that, by 1969, Harry Biggs-Davison has grown from the nervous new boy of 1963 to Head Boy, Captain of soccer and Captain of rugby.) There are long reports of matches and of the sports season in general. (The report of the 1969 rugby season goes on for 2,000 words.) The winner of the Conker Competition is announced each autumn. The Boxing Competition is chronicled, bout by bout. 'L. Cook retired with a damaged eye.' 'Araque retired with a nose-bleed.' Mr Atkinson starts his 'Great Matches of the Past' series, which continues for years (and, naturally, only recalls St Philip's victories). The best of the term's essays by the boys are published, so we can see what a typical prep-school boy in 1968 was thinking about and experiencing.

There was no Mauritius to speak of; no Maldives; no Barbados. 'A Walk on the Downs', 'A Bike Ride in

Herefordshire', and 'The History of Rye' were typical what-I-did-in-my-holidays offerings. It took until 1977 for a boy to write an essay on the thrill of going on holiday in a jumbo jet.

There's a fair amount of moon-interest. 'You are Commander Alan Bean of Apollo 12. Describe your 24 hours before lift-off' was one essay title in January 1970. The school conducted a 'Gallup poll' in January 1969. Favourite football team: Chelsea, 52 votes, Spurs second with 12. Favourite comic: the *Beano*. How interested are you in space travel? Very interested, 59. Quite interested, 12.

Each issue contained a quiz. 'What is the difference between Sir Alf Ramsey and the Most Reverend Michael Ramsey?' 'Do you prefer (a) Bridget Bardot, (b) Raquel Welch, (c) Ursula Andress, (d) Mr Heath?' 'What was the name of Zeus's wife?' 'Why does Concorde's nose go up and down?' 'Name the six countries of the Common Market.' 'Which famous Negro "pop" star recently died?'

Politics made its presence felt in the background. Adrian Barran was losing sleep over atomic war, and wrote a heartfelt treble-voiced plea in the May 1971 issue in a Letter to the Editor: 'I think we ought now to make an international Treaty against atomic war of the future. We must stop it now before it gets too late.'

The Editorial of 1972 predicted a new way of life on joining the Common Market: 'We will be rubbing shoulders with Italian engineers eating German sausages in French cafés in Scunthorpe.' In 1973 Niall Shanahan wrote a poem about the Three-Day Week. One boy was sad about a new flyover. In his poem 'Death of Paddington Green', he wrote this mournful couplet:

> In olden times such a pleasant sight,
> But now cometh the motorway blight.

'May the spirit of Bilbo Baggins [ran a 1974 Editorial] see us all safely through the winter ahead, come elections, come strikes, come food-shortages, come inflation and mass-unemployment. It is much more important that the senior boys pass their Common Entrance and beat Willington at soccer, and that the juniors don't lose their gym shoes.' No change there, then; except that gym shoes would now be called trainers.

School magazines of today adopt a reverential tone towards pupils and their achievements. They have turned into annual prospectuses, glossy marketing tools to attract parents. They lie around on drawing-room coffee tables, ablaze with photographs of children winning prizes, or dressed up on World Book Day, or squinting on the ski-trip. As you flick through them, you are bombarded with vicarious success and happiness.

The tone of the early *Three Stars* magazines of the 1970s is quite different. The boys are regarded simply as boys, with all the flaws and messiness you would expect. The annual trip to London Zoo is described thus: 'There they all were: eating, drinking, playing, fighting, leaping and roaring in their usual profusion: so much for the boys, but the animals were worth watching too.' The 1975 cricket season: 'Played 7, lost 7 – such is the melancholy record of St Philip's 1975. The highest score of the season was 24 . . . The batsmen simply wafted their bats at the ball, for all the world as if they were giving catching practice.' The Common Entrance trials of 1972: 'It is certainly a trial to all concerned, but it is neither common, nor would it guarantee entrance to anywhere but a school whose headmaster had a maniacal zeal to save lost souls.' Art lessons: 'If Pharaoh thought he had problems when the waters of Egypt turned to blood, he never took Remove art.' A replacement maths teacher: 'We welcome Mr Lowe, who is kindly casting pearls before innumerate swine during the unfortunate illness of Mr Hook.' Cricket coaching:

Grave Milward knows he's far from Heaven
Trying to coach our First Eleven.

You can imagine 1970s boys giggling over this stuff. There are a few coy references to skirts, too, which must have seemed quite risqué. 'We congratulate Mr Irvine for growing a moustache in the holidays, as he couldn't afford razor blades after buying a new Mini (car, not skirt).' Thanks are given to Miss Marshall, 'she of the suede mini-skirt, who has taken over the job with cool efficiency' (1973). A year later, fashions have changed: mention is made of the maxi-skirt worn by the new Form 4 teacher, Mrs Goulden. I don't think school magazines of today would get away with such skirt-mentionings.

Coyness about female matters in general (skirts, pregnancy, marriage) was very much a feature of 1970s St Philip's. 'When I joined the school,' Denise Bolam told me, 'there was another female teacher called Vivienne Cartier, from the Cartier family. She married and got pregnant, and when she told David Atkinson about the pregnancy, he said to her, "You'd better leave by Christmas, before it starts to show. We don't want to upset the boys." We all accepted that.' In this bachelor-run environment, a P. G. Wodehousian embarrassment surrounded anything to do with childbirth or romance.

Mr Irvine's engagement and wedding were described thus: 'Robert Irvine has finally fallen for the fairer sex and actually married one of them. Strong men wept.'

*

'Hooky' became the maths teacher for ten years, replacing old Mr Lavender. Mr Hook, a railway enthusiast who came in by train from Aldershot, was partially deaf (deaf enough to miss fire practices) and couldn't keep order. 'I've got no idea how I managed to become a banker, having been taught by him,' one of Mr Hook's ex-pupils, now a high-powered investment banker, told me. 'He completely confused me about maths.'

Stephen de la Bedoyère arrived in 1974 to teach French, starting on a salary of £1,000 a year, and staying for twelve years. Though his surname is French, his voice is upper-class English. 'My first experience was of Timmy barking at me during my interview,' he told me, as we sat in his 1930s mansion flat in Balham.

'Were you a good French teacher?' I asked him.

'Well, it's difficult to teach French well. I was perfectly adequate. We got boys through their Common Entrance.'

'Which other teachers did you admire?'

'Mrs Tolmie was the really charismatic teacher. She gave each boy a different Latin exercise to do at their own level. She knew all the Catholic gossip.' And then he recalled the Great Falling Tree Incident.

It happened during lunch. Mrs Tolmie was serving out the puddings when a tree in the garden fell down and smashed through the window. There was a roar of smashing glass and smashing plates. No one was hurt, fortunately. Mrs Tolmie looked up, and then just carried on serving out the puddings. The best thing about it for the boys was that Mr Atkinson announced, 'Boys, you don't have to finish your fruit salad today.'

De la Bedoyère gave me a striking list of high-profile assassinations, or attempted ones, of members of St Philip's families. 'I was there on the day when a bomb was put under Sir Hugh Fraser's car in Campden Hill Square.' (The bomb killed a kind passer-by, the cancer researcher Professor Gordon Hamilton-Fairley, who had noticed something odd about the car and stopped to have a look.) 'Hugh came straight to St Philip's to reassure his son Orlando that he was alive in case he'd heard about it on the news. We also had a boy whose Spanish grandfather was murdered by ETA. Another boy's father was Mayor of Tehran at the time of the Islamic Revolution, and was executed.'

The exotic foreign Catholic families at the school

fascinated Mr de la Bedoyère, and still fascinate him in his retirement. He also has vivid recollections of Mrs Tibbits's rudeness about foreigners. 'We had a German boy called Mosbacher – known as 'Mossy' – who simply refused to play football. His mother pleaded and pleaded with the school and Mossy got his way. When Mrs Tibbits heard of this, she said, "Typical KRAUTS!"'

*

To this day, Dominic Beddow can remember the early 1970s weekly lunch menu. He gave it to me in full:

Monday: spam, mash (with eyes) and Russian salad – a *déjà-mangé* blend of diced carrot, beetroot chunks, processed peas and salad cream.

Tuesday: uncooked pastry pie with a smear of grey mince within, mash (with eyes) and cabbage.

Wednesday: a meat soup – glutinous and often with pearl barley in it. Plus mash, of course.

Thursday: Maybe liver with tubes, maybe even some roast potato. Or steak and kidney.

Friday: Fish pie with bones.

Never: spaghetti, rice (except pudding), or anything the least bit spicy. No onions. No ice cream, no fresh fruit.

His contemporary Michael Phelan remembers seeing Dominic Beddow being made to sit in the hall all afternoon in front of his cabbage. We now know the reason for no onions: a Mr Atkinson stipulation. And Roger Taylor explained to me the reason for the lack of anything spicy: 'Mrs Tibbits wouldn't touch curry after India, having seen a coolie holding two potatoes between his toes to peel them.'

The food came up on a lift from the basement kitchen to what is now the art room on the ground floor. (As it came trundling up, Roger Taylor would ask, 'And what gastronomic *tour de force* awaits our delectation?') Mrs Bolam described the system to me.

The staff served out the food here, under the window. We taught the boys to have proper table manners. We taught them how to hold a knife and fork. There was no nonsense about not liking things. If a boy said, 'I'm allergic to beetroot', we just said, 'Well, eat it and let's see if you come out in spots.' I remember Whittome did NOT like carrots. But he had to get all of them down. We said to the boys, 'If you were invited to lunch with the Queen, you'd have to eat what you were given, wouldn't you?'

After lunch on games days, everyone got on a coach

to Barnes for games. On the front of one 1970s school magazine, there's a drawing labelled 'Rugby at Harrods'. This surprised me – did they play in the Way In or the Banking Hall? – before I remembered it meant 'the Harrods Ground'. The St Philip's sporting spirit has always been strong, and (being much smaller than other schools) St Philip's teams have always been the underdogs. The natural state of things in the 1970s was to lose matches. 'I actually lost a rugby match 50-nil,' said Benjie Fraser. 'St Philip's broke every prep-school record for being beaten. But we were terribly positive, despite being flattened. We did think we had an edge over Westminster Cathedral Choir School, because they had to protect their precious voices and couldn't shout.' Against Donhead in 1977 St Philip's first cricket eleven were all out for 9. Sports masters tried to be as upbeat as possible in their sports reports. 'As 0-3 defeats go, it was one of the best I've known.'

I've read every school magazine from 1968 to the present day, and have lost count of the number of times St Philip's has lost to Willington. After reading a few issues, I took to just scanning down the sports-results page for the capital 'W' for Willington, and, sure enough – St Philip's had usually lost. There must have been a great many morning-after black moods for Mr Atkinson. It's no wonder that he felt compelled to start his 'Great Matches of the Past' series, in which he dredged up past glories.

But the jubilation at the occasional wins was all the greater. 'A good football season for the first time in years!' ran a headline in 1976. 'Won 6, drawn 2, lost 4.' And on the rare occasions when St Philip's beat Willington, there was (and still is) an air of festival for days.

*

What was it about Roger Taylor that made him such a great man? Every now and then an institution needs someone new to come in and to see the point of it, to tweak it, to make fun of it, to make its people laugh and bring them together. What Roger Taylor brought to the school, in essence, was love.

He had three towering characteristics. He was (a) extremely clever, a polymath, (b) funny and a good writer who never used exclamation marks, and (c) a genuine liker and understander of boys.

During his twenty-three years at the school, the *Three Stars* ended with a column called 'Up Philippi' (inspired by *Up Pompeii*) written by him; and these columns are so good, so irreverent and so eloquent that you dread them coming to an end – rather as one used to dread Alistair Cooke's weekly *Letter from America* coming to an end, which it inevitably did.

Taylor came from a long and august tradition of untrained teachers. I took the train to Oxford to have lunch with him in a pub (not a gastro-pub, just an ordinary urban pub in a backstreet – and it turned out to be a liquid lunch). He was about two feet taller than me, moustachioed, and he wore a hat with a feather and natural history badges sewn on to it, saying things like 'Lyme Regis Museum' and 'I love trilobites'. He wore a cravat and had a hanky sticking out of his leather-jacket pocket. He told me just how untrained as a teacher he was.

I'd got an Exhibition to University College, Oxford, where I read Law. That was the first mistake. I came down with a Second. I did accountancy for two years but I couldn't stand it. I applied for the job at St Philip's in 1967, and Mr Atkinson asked me at the interview, 'What do you want to teach?' 'History and English,' I said. But he asked me to teach Latin. I said I could probably do it with a bit of mugging up. Borrow a few textbooks, it would all come back to me.

I asked him, 'Do prep schools do science?' He said, 'No, but we're going to have to: it's coming into Common Entrance.' I said, 'I'll get you started.'

And that was the beginning of the Science Cupboard. The top three classes came into school on Saturday mornings and did science with Roger Taylor from 10 till noon. 'He was the boys' hero,' Guy de Lotbinière told me. 'His science lessons on Saturday morning were fantastic. We'd make gunpowder. The culmination of every Saturday morning was that he'd drop a wedge of sodium into a large water vessel and it would spin around and explode. He knew how to teach in a way that made us remember everything.' 'No safety goggles to speak of,' Luke Mugliston told me. 'I remember a near-gassing incident with chlorine.'

'I had no formal qualifications in science,' Roger Taylor told me. 'Not so much as an O level. When a boy passed his Common Entrance I said, "You are now, on paper, more qualified than I." I console myself that Darwin and Newton never had any official science education either. Gradually I extended science down the school. I also taught English to the top year because the English teacher didn't like teaching poetry comprehensions. And I taught maths to the 10- to 11-year-olds. I loved that. Just the right age: they weren't silly little boys any more but nor were they goofy teenagers. I always started with a historical introduction to maths. The Ancient Greeks. Euclid. Why the Greeks thought maths so important. Later, when I was teaching them about bearings, I'd illustrate it with the hunt for the *Bismarck*. They learned the whole history of the *Bismarck* as well as how to do bearings.'

Yes, I could see what a good teacher he must have been. Boys, he said to me as he started his second pint, have been the same since they came out of the caves. 'Always kids, playing with the newest things.' He himself, though, is not an embracer of modern technology. 'I do own one of these horrible things [he took out a mobile telephone] but I've probably spent less than £5 on it in three years. I've lost the primer lead.' (He meant 'the charger'.)

Lovingly, in his termly 'Up Philippi' columns, he punctured pomp. 'D. R. Atkinson [he wrote, in one of his columns] has written another publication which sums up the totality of human knowledge of the Clay Pipes of Lesser Uffington. Our Editor, John Theologicus Milward (whom God preserve) is already on the forty-third volume of his 'Life of Blessed Wilhelmina-in-the-Water-Closet.' At the arrival of a new French master Jean-Paul Pichon, he wrote, 'All these French chappies seem to have double-barrelled Christian names. I suppose it makes up for their having guillotined all their own aristocracy. This hirsute pocket-Hercules of the Under-11s seems more like a throwback to Cro-Magnon man. He should feel at home here.' And, when Harry Biggs-Davison joined the staff in 1978, after getting his degree at Cambridge, he was welcomed as 'Harry, the latest exhibit in the staffroom menagerie'.

6

Filofax Mothers

In 1979 we have the first mention in the *Three Stars* of the word 'super-hero'. It's in a story called 'I Was Spiderman'. The 1980s are upon us. Margaret Thatcher is 'in', much to the relief of Harry Biggs-Davison who, during 1980s election campaigns, sticks a 'Maggie in!' poster on to the staffroom wall. There's a genuine fear that, if Maggie is not 'in', private schools will be abolished by a Labour government. An unexpected war breaks out in a faraway country, inspiring boys to write breathless first-person stories. 'The next day, we had to land and start advancing towards Port Stanley.'

One or two hearty traditions are clamped down on. Water pistols (due to the invention of the giant 'super-soaker' version) are banned from the Box Hill outing. Boxing ceases to be an obligatory sport. Modern items make their way into the school's vocabulary. The word 'computer' is first mentioned in summer 1983. (Should the school acquire one? Absolutely not, according to the old guard.) An 'Ansafone' follows shortly after.

The big change in the early 1980s is that mothers start getting involved. Mothers! We know how little time Mr Atkinson and Mrs Tibbits had for mothers: interfering busybodies, who ring up at inconvenient times complaining about 'injustices' and suggesting 'improvements'. Once, when a mother rang up during a staff lunch at Christmas to complain about something, Mr Atkinson simply jumped up and down on the telephone. Mothers were not warmly welcomed when they started the Parents' Association in 1982. But they were unstoppable.

Mothers from 1934 up till now had been unobtrusive sorts, happy to send their sons to St Philip's – or Tibbits' – and simply be at home in the afternoon to welcome them and give them tea. They knew their sons were getting a good Catholic education, and that was what mattered. Their boys went on to Downside, Ampleforth, Worth, Beaumont, St Benedict's, all solid Catholic senior schools, and that was fine. A few mothers worked; most didn't; and the non-working mothers' free time was happily spent shopping, lunching with friends, reading, sewing, gardening, writing thank-you letters and doing good works for the parish.

But now a new generation of mothers was coming into being: highly educated women with degrees from good universities, who either still had a high-powered career, or had given one up in order to devote themselves to motherhood full-time. Ambitious energy was pent up inside them, seeking release. It was not enough just to say goodbye to their sons at the school door and have them back, educated, five years later. They wanted to make the school better: better-equipped, more up-to-date, more high-achieving. They set to work.

The new Parents' Association page in the *Three Stars* of Easter 1982 makes, it has to be said, dull reading. The magazine had always been the preserve of boys and boyish schoolmasters. It had gushed, unembarrassed, with football, cricket and rugby reports, conker competitions, boxing, squad cup winners, boys' stories, Mr Milward's travel adventures, and Mr Taylor's columns and cartoons. Now the mothers came along and started putting in – of all things – advertisements. 'For sale: Perspex coffee table.' (Out with the 1970s.) The new parents' page was littered with bossy underlining: '2.30–3.30 *prompt*.' 'Please put *Saturday 19th May* very firmly in your diaries.' We can hear the unmistakable, rasping sound of one efficient mother reminding other more forgetful mothers to do something. It's a new and slightly grating voice in the St Philip's world – and you can, perhaps, see why Mr Atkinson's staffroom poster (if he had put one up) would have read, 'Mothers out!'

Nor did it take long for the Parents' Association to introduce the inevitable, sensible, machine-washable but unflattering item of sports clothing, the sweatshirt.

*

Young Harry Biggs-Davison was the golden boy of the staffroom. Tall, handsome, a natural at geography-teaching, a dedicated games master, a fervent and kind Catholic, a keen follower of the turf, a player of ping-pong on the staffroom table, loved by staff and pupils, he was mercilessly (but lovingly) teased by Roger Taylor as 'He Who Can Do No Wrong' and 'He Who Has His Finger In Every Pie'. He most certainly was invited to Mrs Tibbits's tea at the end of the school day, and given the prime slice of cake.

And when a beautiful Polish princess called Anna Czartoryska came to teach at the school during Mrs Sayers's maternity leave, and she and Harry fell in love, it made fairy-tales seem possible.

It was not Mrs Tibbits's idea of a fairy-tale, though. 'In Mrs Tibbits's opinion,' Catherine Sayers told me, 'no one was good enough for Harry. Mrs Tibbits adored him. In the end she rather ungraciously accepted that his life was his own.'

Anna Czartoryska – now Anna Biggs-Davison, and Form 4 teacher – showed me the faultlessly polite letter she received from Mr Atkinson in October 1980 offering her a six-month job 'while Mrs Sayers is away for two terms having her baby'. 'Perhaps you would be good enough to let me know in writing as soon as possible your decision.'

'On my first day at the school,' she told me, 'I asked David Atkinson for a curriculum. He looked thoroughly puzzled. I went to a cupboard and found some crumbling old textbooks – and decided just to teach, textbookless. It was some of the best teaching I ever did.'

Carrying on the St Philip's tradition of mispronunciation of foreign surnames, Mr Atkinson called her 'Miss Carter-ouska'. That was quickly changed to 'Miss Ouchamacoucha' by Roger Taylor. She stayed for the stipulated six months, and left, and it was after this that the courtship happened. In the 1982 *Three Stars*, the engagement was announced. And Roger Taylor wrote (in Wodehousian vein):

Yes, our Beloved Editor, He Who Has His Finger In Every Pie, Lord of All He Surveys, Scholar, Punter, and Hearty Young Fool, has cast aside the things of childhood and become engaged. And not only that. Not for him some unacclaimed actress or unclaimable socialite, who would pluck him from our midst; no; he, the most eligible bachelor ever to found the Thursday Hobbies Evening, has selected from the wealth before him not only the winner of the 2.30 at Newmarket, but also our very own Miss Ouchamacoucha.

Again, strong men wept. This time they were joined by strong women.

Mrs Tibbits's father had advised his daughter never to marry a teacher. Anna Czartoryska's mother advised Harry to become a stockbroker 'so you can keep my daughter in comfort rather than in poverty as a schoolmaster'. Neither of these two pieces of parental advice made any difference.

*

Sudden, miraculous flowerings happen. Flemish painting in the 1400s; music in Venice in 1610; art in 1900s Vienna. At St Philip's there was a miraculous flowering of sport in the early 1980s.

It made Mr Atkinson's long, hard slog of a schoolmaster's life worthwhile.

Thirty years later, I interviewed three heroes of this flowering; and they remember the triumphs as if they had happened yesterday. They also gave me fresh insights into Mr Atkinson's carrot-and-stick methods, and his competitiveness against rival schools.

The three best players of the day, on a games afternoon, were given a lift back to school in Mr Atkinson's car. A perk worth striving for, Jasper Arnold told me, because he stopped at the petrol station on the way back and bought the three boys sweets. And if the St Philip's team beat another school in a match, they were all let off homework that evening.

Those were the carrots. Paul Flynn told me about the various varieties of stick. 'Mr Atkinson literally had a stick. He used to march up and down the sideline with his stick and his dog Timmy, watching our every move.'

Rather as the English cricket season always opens with a county playing against an Oxbridge team, the St Philip's football season always opened with a match against the Putney Scouts. It was a warm-up match, not listed as a fixture. 'And in 1980 we beat the Putney Scouts 4-0,' Paul Flynn (now an anaesthetic medical consultant) told me. 'Mr Atkinson was delighted. The next match was against Glengyle, away – if you can call "away" the other side of the Harrods ground. We lost 2-0. Mr Atkinson was incredibly angry. He told us we'd definitely be having homework that night. He stormed into the changing-room and ordered us to go outside and line up by the goal.'

(What would happen next? I couldn't help seeing, once again, Saddam Hussein in my mind's eye, notorious for his post-defeat punishments.)

'We had to put our arms behind our backs. Then Mr Atkinson just kicked balls at us. Hard. We had to deflect them. He split us into two groups and made us carry on kicking balls at each other, for ages. It was to show us we'd been weak, namby-pamby. It was to show us we weren't to shirk.'

And from that moment on, St Philip's won every game of the season. 'Except the away match against Willington. But he didn't make us do homework on the evening when we lost that one. And in the last match of the season, we beat Willington at home! We played our socks off. Mr Atkinson was so happy.'

At last he could stop having to relive Great Matches of the Past, and could bask in Great Matches of the Present.

Mr Atkinson got very excited on the day when the photographer came to take the team photograph. 'I told him I had a maths exam that day,' Paul Flynn said, 'and he said, "Well, you'll just have to come out of the exam half an hour early, won't you?"' Nothing was going to get in the way of immortalizing this winning team. 'Lavradio had forgotten his kit. Atkinson was furious. They had to find a spare one – and the only one they could find belonged to the smallest boy in the school. They had to pin the school colours on to it. You can see the photo on the wall: I look stressed because I've come out of an unfinished maths exam, and Lavradio looks in agony, squeezed into a tiny yellow shirt with pins digging into his chest.'

'Prepare for the worst. Hope for the best.' That, Luke Mugliston told me, was Mr Atkinson's motto. After years of having to rely on the first half of the motto, the second half suddenly seemed relevant. A rich seam of sporting high-achievers had arrived at the school: boys so talented that they were spotted and put in the first team by the age of 10 or 11. So keen were these boys on cricket that the mother of one of them – Sue Arnold, now the school's housekeeper – took them to Hyde Park every Saturday morning and left them there to practise cricket all day.

'With a packed lunch?' I asked.

'We were too busy playing to eat,' Jasper retorted. 'When I first came to the school and saw the trophy cabinet, I thought, "I want that one, that one, that one, that one and that one."'

This ambition and practising fervour led to the first-ever century. Summer 1983, against Westminster Cathedral Choir School: Jasper Arnold scored it; and his batting partner Luke Mugliston scored 33. The school had come a long way from being all out for 9 against Donhead.

That Donhead defeat rankled with Mr Atkinson. Again, we get a glimpse of the way in which his prickly competitiveness went hand in hand with deep kindness. The reason why Paul Flynn came to St Philip's was that he had been asked to leave Donhead – the Jesuit school in Wimbledon – because his brother had left to go to an Anglican school. (When I asked Paul Flynn whether he remembered corporal punishment at St Philip's, he said, 'It was very tame compared with Donhead, where they still used the ferula.')

'Mr Atkinson was very keen to have me at St Philip's, because Donhead was such a rival. At the entry test he just handed me a book and asked me to read a page. I did, and he said, "Right: you're in."'

The change of schools at the age of 10 was traumatic. Paul went into a kind of depression. 'I cried all the time. I couldn't settle. And Mr Atkinson helped me through it. At least once a day, for the whole of my first two terms, I was in tears and was allowed out of class to go and see him. You never knocked on his door. You climbed on to a step and looked through a little glass hatch. He'd see you, and come round and open the door. He talked to me and calmed me, every single day. He never lost patience. And at the end of the year he created a new cup for me: the Young Footballer of the Year cup. "We'd like to present this to someone who might have been crying all year, but who has also been our most outstanding young footballer." From that moment on I was never depressed again.'

And Mr Milward, in his end-of-term report for Paul, wrote, 'I hope he leaves brooding to hens.'

*

Foreign-surname mispronunciation was reaching chronic levels. In the early 1980s, there was a large influx of Arabs into the school, as well as the usual mix of glamorous Europeans. The English were heavily outnumbered. 'Hello to Lam I, Al-Saheal, Castillo, Latipi, O'Broin, Roberts II, Hopkirk, Constantini, Vega, Kelly, Marmarchi I and II, Deutsch and Castella,' says the Christmas 1981 *Three Stars*. One of the glamorous Muslims had a mother whose correct title was 'The Begum'. 'Beggum?' asked Mrs Tibbits, disdainfully. 'What's this Beggum?' Another boy was called Fatimi, with the emphasis on the second syllable. Mrs Tibbits called him, simply, 'Fatima'.

St Philip's has always been tolerant of and welcoming to non-Catholics. In the early 1980s, it had to be. 'Until the Second Vatican Council,' Harry Biggs-Davison told me, 'it was almost a commandment of the Church that Catholic children should go to a Catholic school. That all changed in the early 1970s. Catholic families started sending their sons to other schools, and St Philip's didn't do anything to address this. It just soldiered on.'

The non-marketing Mr Atkinson accepted all comers, and the local wealthy Arab population readily filled the spaces. But numbers were going steadily down. Big prep schools with marketing departments were opening all over London, pulling in boys by the hundreds, promising parents they would get their sons into trophy non-Catholic senior schools. 'Other schools were doing posher things on posher premises,' as Roger Taylor put it. 'In 1981 our numbers were down to 72,' Harry Biggs-Davison said, 'and the school was in danger of closing.'

This brought on the staffroom row that changed everything.

Harry continued:

Mrs Bolam and I had a quick meeting before the staff meeting in September 1981, and said to each other, 'Something has got to be done.' At the meeting, David Atkinson was talking about having to make members of staff redundant. We said, 'This is rubbish. You don't just allow people to lose their jobs.' David said, 'Well you can all go to bloody hell and I'll close the school now.' And he stormed out of the room. Mrs Tibbits shouted at me. I went down to the flat [where Mr Atkinson and Mrs Tibbits lived] and apologized to David. He said, 'I know you're right. We should do something – but I haven't got a clue how to go about it.' And I – as the 25-year-old who had the answer to everything – talked to him about marketing, and talking to parents and other schools, about networking and contacts. From that moment on David gave me carte blanche to take charge of the marketing side of things, and to make suggestions about what changes we should make.

As soon as Harry took over as 'admissions headmaster', numbers went up. Paula Chandler, who arrived as secretary to Mr Atkinson in 1982 and still plays the piano for Assembly every morning, told me, 'In my first term we got the numbers up from 74 to 82. I was proud of that. Show-rounds were important to Harry. And I was front-of-house.'

Gone was the cap of one set of parents per week, allowed a tour only after closing time. Now, escorted by Harry, two sets of prospective parents came during every day to be given a glimpse of the vibrancy of school life as it happened. The larger London schools, tapping into the new mass panic among middle-class parents, had to resort to giant 'open mornings' on Saturdays, when 200 parents at a time were shunted round the school by acceptable top-year boys. Set against this, the individual showing-round by Harry Biggs-Davison became (and remains) something to treasure.

The school's aspirations crept up as well. 'At St Philip's I learned that losing is a very distant second to actually winning,' said Luke Mugliston, who went on to be a member of the British fencing team and to win a silver medal for England at the Commonwealth Games. 'And when three of us got into Westminster and St Paul's in 1985, it felt as if the school was getting the bunting out. There was a real air of celebration.'

The other 'noose hanging round the school's neck', as Harry described it to me, was that the building was jointly owned by Mrs Tibbits and Mr Atkinson, and if one of them died, there would have been an extortionate amount of inheritance tax to pay, which would have forced the school to close.

Strangely enough, it was an admission of anxiety about this from Mrs Tibbits during a physiotherapy session that set in motion a chain of events which averted this impending disaster. Mrs Tibbits had a bad back, and her physiotherapist was Barbara Doherty, whose son Justin had been at St Philip's in the late 1960s. Barbara came home to Barnes one day after one of the physiotherapy sessions, and said to her husband Dr Peter Doherty, 'Mrs Tibbits is very worried about what will happen to the school when she dies.' 'Is she?' said her husband. And he got thinking.

Within days, he had started to do something about it. He got together a group of St Philip's parents and ex-parents who loved the school, and they decided that in order to secure the school's future they should buy it from Mr Atkinson and Mrs Tibbits, and turn it into a charitable trust. This they did, with a generous loan from the Midland Bank and a generously low asking price from Mrs Tibbits and Mr Atkinson. On becoming a charitable trust, St Philip's was exempt from inheritance tax, and the noose hanging round its neck was gone.

For the first time, it now had a board of school governors. During Mr Tibbits's day, the school had not had governors but 'patrons' – a list of prestigious Catholics on the school's letterhead: 'The Cardinal Archbishop of Westminster, the Right Reverend the Abbot of Downside, the Right Reverend the Abbot of Worth, the Right Reverend the Abbot of Ampleforth, the Rector of Stonyhurst, the Supervisor of the Oratory, the Abbot of Ealing, the Countess of Long-ford, Sir John Biggs-Davison MP, Lord Forte,' etc. These 'patrons' were powerless to make decisions on school-management matters: they were there purely to lend tone. Mr Tibbits wouldn't have liked governors. He was headmaster and board of governors combined. Dr Doherty became the first chairman of the new board of real governors and remained in the post for twenty years. And his files (which he showed me at his dining-room table, the scene of many riotous gover-nors' meetings) make riveting reading.

*

Though she was growing old, Mrs Tibbits continued to keep an iron grip on the way things were done, at a domestic level at least. Female teachers were still firmly kept out of the staffroom. 'Women had to go up to where the piano was,' Catherine Sayers told me, 'near the boys' loos. We just sat there, freezing cold. Some-how we didn't mind.' At Christmas, the female mem-bers of staff got a card from Mrs Tibbits, while she gave the men MCC diaries.

In her nylon housecoat, chain-smoking Benson & Hedges, Mrs Tibbits presided over the ground-floor corridor, and nothing escaped her eye. 'She was the

scariest chain-smoking person I've ever met,' Paul
Flynn said. 'You just tried to avoid being around her.
Once I heard one of the teachers ask her about her
smoking habit. She said, "I've been doing it for 60
years and I'm not dead yet."'

But even people like Mrs Tibbits fade eventually;
and the 1980s was the decade of her fading. You can
sense it coming. She begins to be mentioned in the
Three Stars as a kind of national treasure – more Queen
Mother than Margaret Thatcher. When she is awarded
the Pope's *Bene Merenti* medal in 1983 she attains a new
haloed status. 'The great honour bestowed on her by
Cardinal Hume, on behalf of His Holiness the Pope,
was a source of great pride and joy to us all at St
Philip's' says the *Three Stars* editorial of 1983; and to
this day you can see the photograph of this medal-
bestowing on the school staircase. Bright-eyed, smiling
a Queen-Motherly, closed-mouth smile, elegantly
dressed, she looks almost royal and you would never
guess at her housecoat and Benson & Hedges way of
life. She was awarded the medal for maintaining St
Philip's as a Catholic school all those years, after the
death of her husband. The hymns at Assembly (thanks
to Mr Atkinson's Anglican tastes) were now of the
staunch 'Onward, Christian Soldiers' variety; but still,
the general ethos was as Catholic as could be. Father

Keely, the school's chaplain from the Carmelite Church, prepared the younger boys for First Communion and the older boys for Confirmation; and in this way Mr Tibbits's original vision for the school was kept alive.

Cardinal Hume towered over Mrs Tibbits and he had to bend a long way down to try to pin the *Bene Merenti* medal on to her woollen jacket. She snatched it out of his hand and said (with a hint of snappiness in her voice), 'I can do it myself, thank you very much!'

Every year, Mrs Tibbits had judged the annual art competition. But in 1983, she suddenly didn't. Then, at Easter 1984, the school was 'wishing Mrs Tibbits a speedy recovery from her recent illness'. She was in St Stephen's Hospital with a chest complaint. She recovered; but, as Roger Taylor told me, 'Poor dear Mrs Tibbits was getting a bit out of it, dropping her ash in the mashed potatoes and thinking that David was giving the school away.'

Then in 1984 she retired as housekeeper – and Sue Arnold took over, remaining in the post to this day. Spam was never seen again. Spaghetti Bolognese made its first appearance. And Mrs Arnold spoke the immortal words, 'It's counter-productive to make children eat everything on their plate if you have to clear up the sick afterwards.' The eating-everything rule, which had darkened so many childhoods, was instantly relaxed.

And a quiet word from Harry Biggs-Davison to Mr Atkinson brought an instant end to corporal punishment. Harry explained that it simply wasn't in fashion any more.

Mr Atkinson agreed to his becoming joint headmaster in 1984. This was Roger Taylor's reaction in 'Up Philippi':

It's that man again. Our Distinguished Editor. He-who-has-his-finger-in-every-pie. What is he now? Only Assistant Head, isn't he? Can't you see the inevitable rise ahead? Absolute ruler of the whole known universe? It has to come. And the timing of it! 1984, of course. His master plan unfolds. Poor old D. R. A.: another Hindenburg bowing before the meteoric rise of the new order.

Mr Atkinson took a 'semi-sabbatical leave': but not before appointing Sue Arnold (mother of three St Philip's boys) to be his aunt's successor as housekeeper. Sue Arnold remembers him offering her the post: 'Mrs Arnold: we need a lady at the helm. Your boys are going off to public school, which is going to cost you a lot of money. You'll need a job.' She has now done the job for twenty-eight years.

'David's a wonderful man,' she told me. (The present tense almost shocked me. But we must remember, Mr Atkinson is alive and living on the South Coast. He just prefers not to see anyone. Mrs Arnold once drove there and knocked on his door unannounced. He was mortified. Roger Taylor said to me, 'If God knocked on the door, David would say, "Not today, thank you."') 'He had a black-and-white television for decades,' Sue Arnold said. 'I think he's only just gone over to colour. His dogs were his family. I remember once asking him, "How's Tim today?" He replied, "He's got a bit of an upset tummy after I gave him a bone." To this day I've never told him I was in fact asking about my son who was a pupil at the school.'

*

The Great Computer Debate rolled on, filling the parents' page of the *Three Stars*. To acquire one or not to acquire one? The progressive mothers wrote, 'It would be a pity if a situation were to develop in which pupils became more knowledgeable than their teachers in such an important field as computer science.' The more old-fashioned mothers wrote, 'Is it wise, or even sensible, to jump on the computer bandwagon just for the sake of it, before we know the full implications of the future role of computers in schools?'

The school did a survey of eleven other independent schools to find out what they were doing. Ten of the schools had already installed a computer. One headmaster complained that 'the children are so busy queuing to play with the computer that they are neglecting their other studies'. Another school, with a BBC computer, Model B, was having servicing difficulties.

The general consensus was that, if a computer were introduced, 'it would be as a hobby rather than an aid to studies'. The progressive mothers won, and the £900 raised at the first-ever summer fair in 1984 (at which Roger Taylor drew funny faces of people at 30p a go) went towards the school's first-ever computer – 'a brand-new BBC "B" micro-computer'. Soon after came an Amstrad word-processor, with ugly rounded squares for 'o's'. The Parents' Association had the wind in their sails, and the chairwoman, Gabrielle Leigh-Wood, now launched a £300,000 appeal to raise money for improvements.

Mrs Tibbits was unable to attend sports day in 1984: she was now at a nursing home in West Sussex. We hear her sending her last thanks to the school for cards and good wishes; and then, early in 1986, she dies. Roger Taylor, as always, has the apposite words.

The day we heard of her death, the school had run out of a certain vital commodity. The world cried, 'It would not have happened in Mrs Tibbits's day.' She would have put it more concisely: 'Tiresome.'

He also put on record that she had said these words to him, about the boys in the school: 'Of course, I love them all really; but don't you dare tell them.'

*

Miss Cramer was dead, worn out in her fifties from good works. Nice old deaf Mr Hook was dead. Mrs Tibbits was dead. But boys carried on being boys, and in the term of Mrs Tibbits's death, D. Zafer, aged 11, enthused about his favourite hobby: pencil-sharpening collecting. 'I get my pencil sharpenings from my friends at school and from my sisters' friends. I put them in bags and tins in big cupboards in my room. I keep a log book of every kind of pencil sharpening I collect. The rarest I have is a rubber-pencil sharpening.'

Boys, from the most mainstream to the weirdest, needed to be accommodated and nurtured. One of Mrs Tibbits's catchphrases was brought back to life as a new motto: 'Now we can get ON'.

7

Carmelites and Oratorians

'The best day of my life was when I went to Docklands on a train without a driver.' (C. Bach, aged 10, in 1987.)

Is a child's excitement about a ride on the new Docklands Light Railway quaint enough to count as history? Just, perhaps. I've heard it said that you need at least twenty years of perspective in order to sort out the historically interesting from the historically dull. Here is another almost-quaint vignette from the early 1990s. 'London has become "Continental" [said the *Three Stars* editorial of 1993] with the advent of the street café serving Espresso, Cappuccino, croissants and pastries.' (It's the capital letters and inverted commas that make that sentence historically interesting.)

We're marching towards the present now, and I don't want to bore you with changes of maths teacher, the advent of the annual school play, the switch from a hand-held bell to an electric one, the removal of the old gas fires, the new carpet in the library, or the building of a science lab on the top floor. You get the picture.

It's useful for a biographer if his subject dies young and tragically, rather than doddering on into her nineties like Dodie Smith. (It's not much fun for the subject, though.) St Philip's, thankfully, is still going strong: tricky for its historian but good for the world. I'll run you through the chain of events.

(The new electric bell made a hideous noise, so they went back to using a hand-held one, and what was known as 'the Paula Chandler ringing system': 'I'll ring that bell when I've finished typing this letter.' The new central heating system packed up during 'the coldest November since the last woolly mammoth caught flu'. The carpet in the library caused an outcry: 'Are we no longer to stand on rotting lino, fondly arranging the Sellotape on first editions of *Just William* and *Biggles*?' The brilliant new maths teacher, Mr Walters, clarified the world of algebra to a mystified generation, and continues to do so.)

Roger Taylor lost his faith.

'I was saying the Creed in a school Mass one day,' he told me in the Oxford backstreet pub, 'when I suddenly thought, "Hang on. I don't believe a word of this."'

He admitted as much to the joint headmasters, who received the news with compassion. St Philip's has always been accommodating towards doubters. The Adam-and-Eve/Big Bang dichotomy trod its thin line at St Philip's, as it does in all Christian schools, the science master steering difficult questions away by saying, 'Ask the Religious Knowledge teacher,' and the RK teacher mumbling, 'Ask the science teacher.'

For other reasons entirely, Roger Taylor nearly lost his job. A great man, yes: but not good at keeping discipline. A few old boys had mentioned this to me in passing – 'Fantastic science teacher, brilliant explosions, talked to you as if you were an adult, gave you his liquorice papers to chew, not that great at keeping order' – but it wasn't until I was leafing through a box of papers in the ex-chairman of governors' dining-room in Barnes that I realized how close to the precipice this flaw took him.

'Dear Roger,' ran a letter to him from Mr Atkinson, 'I have told you on many occasions that the children are to sit properly at their desks during lessons, yet I found five of 1B milling about in the room on Tuesday, and caught Peters sticking a pen into Payet's backside right in front of you, which you did not appear to notice.' And, on another occasion: 'This morning I saw

Serasinghe in Remove, right in front of you, putting a plastic mask over his face and grinning at all the other children while you were teaching, following which I saw Troilo reading comic strips on his knee. We regret to say that in this school, this type of conduct is completely unacceptable.' A termination of the contract was threatened.

Roger Taylor pleaded, in an apologetic handwritten reply, 'Any teacher can only teach in accordance with his character. To try to teach in another, albeit "better" way, would simply not work for him.' But he promised to try harder to keep order. The death of his father meant that he had to move to Abingdon to look after his mother, from where he commuted to and from St Philip's each day. The result of this was tiredness, which led to tetchiness, which led to 'a shorter fuse' in science lessons – which saved him.

The truth was, Mr Atkinson was out of his depth in the new post-corporal-punishment world order. This was mentioned in a governors' meeting: 'Conduct is proving a problem for Mr Atkinson, since smoking, drinking and stealing seem to be on the increase and some children these days fear nothing since the abolition of corporal punishment.' Troubles seemed to be coming thick and fast. A boy was expelled for 'an appalling exhibition of rudeness in full view of women and girls at the Chelsea Baths'. Four boys were suspended for a week for 'stealing the badges off Volkswagens, etc, by subterfuge during walks at school breaks'. Two more boys were caught smoking at a bus-stop in Chelsea. Ten more were caught smoking during the Box Hill outing of 1988. A boy was caught with forty pens in his pocket, which he'd shoplifted from Maxwell's. These misdemeanours generated weeks of letters unpleasant to dictate, and replies from parents unpalatable to read. How to put a stop to the new brand of modern, coarse, 1980s naughtiness without instant recourse to the cane? What was needed – and what came later – was an appeal to boys' deeper sense of morality, instilling in them a habit of good behaviour not through fear of corporal punishment but through respect and innate kindness (and a desire to avoid Saturday-morning detention).

*

'A *slight* treading on toes.' This was how Roger Taylor described to me the five-year-long joint headmastership of David Atkinson and Harry Biggs-Davison. An understatement, perhaps. It was not easy for a bright, young, visionary headmaster to share power with his old history master and previous boss, a revered man, but set in his 1950s ways, averse to change, not keen on meeting parents, and having no idea how to raise standards and lift the school's profile.

'Nor can it have been easy for David,' Harry Biggs-Davison said to me, 'having the young pretender butting in all the time. We just about coped.'

The two headmasters and Paula Chandler (the school secretary) shared the tiny headmaster's office: three desks, 'and Paula going out on to the fire escape to have her fag'. There was one shared diary. It was agreed that the non-marketing David Atkinson would interview current parents, and Harry would see prospective parents.

Harry remembers one particular diary entry which gave him new insight into the private habits of his co-headmaster.

'I was trying to fix up a late-afternoon interview with some parents, and saw that David had written in the diary, "5 p.m.: S. T. 6 p.m.: R. F." I told him I wanted to see some parents in the office but had noticed that he'd booked appointments for those times. "Oh, no, no, no," David said, slightly embarrassed. "Those aren't appointments. They're just something private."'

Whom could the initials 'S. T.' and 'R. F.' stand for, Harry wondered? He was intrigued. It wasn't until later, when he was flicking through the *Radio Times*, that he spotted '5.00: *Star Trek*' and '6.00: *The Rockford Files*'.

The dog-walking, the clay-pipe-collecting, the *Star Trek*-in-black-and-white-watching, the plain onion-free diet . . . all these were such quiet habits, and it was always a shock when David Atkinson exploded with sudden high-decibel rage, which he did every now and then.

'It happened one day just as some prospective parents were arriving,' Harry Biggs-Davison told me. 'David was in our office, exploding, shouting his head off. I went downstairs to answer the doorbell, and the parents came in, and you could hear this booming sound coming from the office. I didn't know what to do. I decided to show the parents the art room on the ground floor first, and managed to spin it out, hoping the hubbub would die down.' Ten minutes later it did, and the coast was clear to take the parents up to the office. 'They looked slightly bemused,' Harry recalls.

The arrangement could not go on forever. 'My career at St Philip's can only stagnate', Harry Biggs-Davison wrote to the chairman of the governors after two years of the shared headmastership, 'amidst all the frustrations of my present partnership with the other headmaster.' If nothing changed, he wrote, he would feel obliged to look elsewhere for a job.

We have disgruntled parents to thank for the fact that he stayed rather than left. The final straw for Mr Atkinson was a fracas with a furious mother on the school's front doorstep. In the Lent term of 1989, parents of six boys gave notice. Enough was enough. In August 1989, Mr Atkinson wrote a gracious and pivotal letter to the chairman:

> I have been headmaster for 22 years, the first seventeen on my own, the last five jointly. I reckon I have, at one time or another, done every job it is possible to do in such an establishment. Now I feel very strongly that I should like to give up the pressured responsibilities of being headmaster and opt for a quieter life – i.e. just teaching my history which I enjoy, and nothing else much. I have offered Harry Biggs-Davison, should he take on the sole headmastership, to be his deputy, in case of illness or emergency – but this post is purely nominal.

Or, as the minutes of the next governors' meeting

put it, quoting Mr Atkinson's own words, 'D. R. A. can no longer be bothered with difficult parents, and is finding it a strain. He is retiring as headmaster. He promises not to get under anyone's feet by hovering and making silly suggestions.'

So he resigned the headmastership – but would carry on being a history master for a further nine years. 'Readers of this rubbish over the past few years', wrote Roger Taylor in his 'Up Philippi' column, 'will remember my warnings, my pointing to ominous signs and portents. All has come true, and our glorious leader straddles the school like a Colossus. The first duumvirate is dissolved, and D. R. A., F. S. A. is consigned to that builder's skip of history, namely, the staffroom.'

When people asked Mr Atkinson whether he minded the downgrading from headmaster to mere teacher, he said, 'Well, don't Abbots go back to being simple monks or parish priests quite happily?'

He was never greedy about his status, or about money. He took a drop in salary, and when, a few years later, he moved permanently to the South Coast, he sold his half-share of the flat, 2 Wetherby Place, to Paula Chandler 'for peanuts'. 'He went off with my cheque,' Paula Chandler told me, 'and he used it as a bookmark in his next history lesson.'

*

'It was like a fresh wind blowing into the school,' remembers Abdollah Ghavani (an Iranian, now a Senior Lecturer at London Metropolitan University), speaking of the moment when Harry Biggs-Davison took over as sole headmaster. 'Harry wanted to prove the school's worth, and to raise standards. He wanted students to go to the best senior schools. Suddenly we were aiming high, all working very hard – it was competitive but in a friendly way. The teaching was superb. I went on to Westminster and then Cambridge. Lots of my contemporaries went on like me to follow as careers things they had started to be passionate about at St Philip's.'

Getting-into-private-schools madness was gripping London. It became (and remains) the chief topic of conversation among many middle-class parents and their chief obsession. At conception, babies without names were being put on waiting lists for the best nursery schools – the kind where you start doing worksheets at the age of $2\frac{1}{2}$ – so that they could be assessed at 3 and get into the best pre-prep schools – the kind where you do daily verbal reasoning tests from the age of 5 – so they could get in to the best prep schools at 7-

or 8-plus, so they could get into the best senior schools, so they could get into the best universities, so they could become prematurely grey investment bankers and earn the fees for the next generation. St Philip's found itself becoming one of these sought-after prep schools. Not a bad thing to be, if you're a private establishment trying to stay in the black; but it's never a pleasant task to send letters of rejection to parents, who take such things personally.

'Is there *anything* about you that's Catholic?' pre-prep-school headmistresses asked parents. 'If there is, your son should try for St Philip's . . .'

Scores of nervous 6- and 7-year-old young hopefuls started coming along on the annual Entry Test day, with their hair combed into side partings and wearing their spotless school uniforms, trying their hand at Getting In. Thirty or forty boys sat the entrance exam for eight places – and then went on in droves to sit the Westminster Under School exam, the Colet Court exam, the Sussex House exam, the King's Wimbledon exam, their parents praying that at least one of these would hit the mark. The school's numbers shot up, from the upper eighties to capacity, at 110.

And this growth made the governors want to expand, expand, expand. Why not start a pre-prep school, which would 'feed' straight into the prep school? Then you could catch the best ones young, as so many other schools were doing. Forays were made into finding new premises. The house next door? The old Royal College of Organists beside the Albert Hall? A building in its own grounds in Chiswick? All these possibilities were looked into. A letter to parents in 1993 reassured them that the character of the school would not change if it moved, 'nor is there any possibility of the school going south of the river or north of Hyde Park'. (God forbid.)

But the premises were never found. The closest the school came to moving was when it was the under-bidder for the Marist Convent site in Fulham. The convent announced its imminent closure in 1995. St Philip's was hoping to buy it in conjunction with the girls' school More House, and turn it into a co-educational independent Catholic beacon.

'We thought we had the winning ticket,' Harry Biggs-Davison told me, 'because we went in with a housing association. The plan was to reduce the size of the playground and build local housing.' Surely the nuns would like the idea of this? Surely they would want the institution to remain Catholic? 'We even asked Cardinal Hume to write a letter to the Reverend

Mother pleading on our behalf. He said, "I'll do what I can, but I can tell you it won't make any difference."'

Sure enough, it didn't make any difference. 'The Reverend Mother shut herself into the new premises in New Malden and told the estate agent to take the highest bid,' Harry said. 'We offered nearly £3 million,' Peter Doherty told me, 'and the Girls' Day School Trust offered 4. The nuns went for the money. They said they'd got their "elderly sisters" to care for.' The building became Kensington Prep School for Girls.

Is bigger necessarily better? We know in our hearts that it is by no means so. But businessmen insist that it is. Astonishingly, the school still exists in the house that Mr Tibbits bought in 1934. The continuity produces its own unique atmosphere. The smallness means that all the boys know each other and the headmaster knows them – really knows them. But all around Britain, schools are expanding, merging, becoming parts of chains owned by hedge funds, with logos.

*

The school was still adrift from the Oratory. Since the death of Mr Tibbits in 1967, school Masses had been taking place in the Carmelite Church in Kensington. 'Mass at the Carmelites', Harry Biggs-Davison told me, 'was frankly ghastly.' The church was a great barn of a building, and the whole school only took up the front three rows. The organ was far away at the back, never in time with the singing – and the music was getting trendier by the year.

Father Patrick Keely (about whom Mrs Tibbits had been so withering due to his strong Irish accent) was an extremely kind and good chaplain, and the arrangement, though not perfect, carried on for almost a quarter of a century.

Then the Prior was sent back to Ireland, and Father Patrick was sent to work in Gerrards Cross. The new Prior was to be a man called Father John. Father Patrick's last words to Harry were a warning: 'If you can get out, do.'

Harry soon saw what he meant. Father John turned out to be a hearty middle-aged priest with smelly breath, who said all the right things about how he was looking forward to being the school's chaplain, but was hopeless with children.

He came to look round the school [Harry told me] and I showed him into a classroom. The children stood up, and Father John said [in sing-song Irish accent], 'Why don't you sing a song to me, now?' There was complete silence. The boys had no idea what to sing to him. He pointed to a small black boy in the front row called David Macharia, and said, 'You, there, why don't you sing me a song?' At a loss, David blurted out, 'What about "Baa Baa Black Sheep"?' Father John was horrified. We did eventually manage to cobble together a verse of 'Soul of My Saviour' – though I think Father John would have preferred 'Lord of the Dance'.

Things came to a head at the school carol service at the Carmelite Church – 'the worst school carol service in the history of the world', Harry said. 'First of all, the music was dire. Our head of music at the time liked everyone to perform, whatever their standard. We had a violin solo as a separate item, and the noise of screeching cats was so appalling that parents were seen vacating the church with handkerchiefs stuffed into their mouths.'

Then Father John stood up and gave a firebrand sermon, haranguing the congregation, telling them that they were unhealthily wealthy and should not be indulging themselves in school carol services but giving all their money to the poor. 'It was a left-wing diatribe,'

Harry said. 'That's when Anthony Jeffery said, "I'll try for the Oratory".'

*

Scratch beneath the surface of all these Catholics, and there's quite a lot of recent Anglicanism about. If you had visited Lampeter University in Wales in the early 1980s, you might have come across two young Anglican undergraduate friends both reading Theology: Dominic Jacob, an organ scholar, and Anthony Jeffery, who hoped to become an Anglican priest and had a place at Mirfield, the High Anglican training college in Yorkshire.

Both converted to Catholicism while at Lampeter. Anthony, in his final year, was studying Cardinal Newman 'who persuaded me that that was the way'. He was received into the Catholic Church in Wales, and became a novice at the Birmingham Oratory. Dominic converted at the age of 21. He also joined the Birmingham Oratory, and it was while seeing him taking his vows at his ordination to the diaconate that Anthony thought, 'I just can't do this.' He left, and leaving was traumatic. He came to London, and went to Gabbitas-Thring to see if there were any suitable teaching jobs to be had. There was a vacancy for Head of English at a small Catholic prep school in South Kensington called St Philip's. He arrived to be greeted by boys running in circles round a sleeping Mrs Tolmie, and was shown round by Mr Atkinson, 'who offered me Marmite sandwiches'. He was offered and accepted the job. 'The whole place was slightly mad, but I was used to that, from the Oratory.'

His Oratory connections meant that he could pull strings with the Oratorians. 'Father Richard, the Provost, was the one Oratorian who didn't want us,' Harry recalls. 'He just wanted a quiet life. The other Fathers were happy about having us back.' But with a special plea from Anthony Jeffery, the Provost agreed to 'put it to the Fathers. We got voted in, and suddenly we were welcomed back to the fold.'

But how to break the news to Father John at the Carmelite Church? 'I did the cowardly thing of writing a letter to him,' Harry said. 'I explained that the school had been founded as the school of St Philip Neri, and so on, and told him how profoundly grateful we were to the Carmelites for all they had done for us over the years, but how I hoped that he would understand it was right for us to be reunited with the Oratory. I put a cheque into the envelope, quite a generous donation to the Carmelites.'

He hoped that would be the end of the matter. It wasn't. A few days later he arrived back at the school from the games field and Paula Chandler told him, 'You've got a visitor.'

'Father John was standing up in the office,' Harry said, 'steaming with anger, and waving the cheque around. He'd walked all the way from Kensington Church Street in his full brown Carmelite habit and sandals. He shouted about "ingratitude", and he waved the cheque in the air saying, "Conscience money! It's just conscience money!" He tore the cheque to pieces, and said, "That will be the last you'll be seeing of me, and I hope the last I'll be seeing of you." Then, presumably, he walked all the way back.'

From the moment of rejoining the Oratory, liturgical standards rose as fast as academic ones. Excellence and beauty in school Masses were aimed for. Anthony Jeffery asked his friend Dominic from the Birmingham Oratory to visit the school. He heard confessions, and continued to visit twice a term until 1995, when he became the school's chaplain as well as Religious Knowledge teacher. And in 1998 a brilliant young organist of 23, Charles Cole, fresh out of university, came for an interview for Head of Music.

All three of these new members of staff had high

expectations, liturgically and musically. They were a filter through which nothing shoddy could percolate. The Schola Cantorum was started – the school choir – in which Palestrina was sung, the treble line by the boys, the other three parts by professionals, one to a part. One of the founder members of the Schola was Mica Penniman, who became the pop star Mika. 'That boy's got a voice,' Cardinal Hume said, on hearing him.

*

The day came – it had to come eventually – when Mr Atkinson actually left. He'd first come to the school as a junior PE master in 1952. Now, in 1998, it was time to go. On the very evening that he left the school, he drove down to the South Coast and never came back.

But he forbade any kind of farewell ceremony. He refused a leaving party. His final day was slightly awkward because everybody wanted to say something momentous, but he wouldn't have it. He did accept the offer of choosing his own menu for lunch on his last day. He chose egg and chips.

There was a skip on the street outside his flat. As a way of smothering his emotions, perhaps, Mr Atkinson was ruthless and unsentimental in his throwing away of possessions. 'He was being slightly light-headed about it,' Harry Biggs-Davison said, 'chucking out loads of pictures – even the framed photograph of Mrs Tibbits receiving her Pope's medal. "No use to me any more," he said.'

Having thrown everything out, he drove off, with his Mars Bar, into retirement.

When he'd gone, the staff waving goodbye on the pavement reached into the skip and rescued a large amount of precious stuff before the skip lorry came to take it away.

*

It's a White Shirt Day, in September 2010. Mass at 11.30 in the Little Oratory. The boys are excited because the normal lesson-filled morning is disrupted. They line up in silence and file into the Little Oratory, and their parents (warmly invited to attend school Masses) gaze at them and wonder whether it's too late to have just one more baby. (But it might be a girl.) That blue of the St Philip Neri shield does make a fetching colour for a blazer, and the chestnut-brown panelling behind them makes an aesthetically delightful backdrop. There's the lovely Mrs Hitch, with her little flock of 8-year-olds. There's Mr Mules, the splendid history master and instigator of the Form 7 History trip to Bristol, handing out service sheets. Here comes Mr Milward, the great Latin master, recently retired after 42 years, but he never misses a Mass.

All stand. The organ plays in the gallery. The procession begins, led by Mr Jeffery and the candle-holding boy-servers, following whom comes Father Dominic in his glittering chasuble. You think, 'It's good for boys to be part of this liturgical pomp.' As Father Dominic says, 'The Mass has got to be something they grow into, not grow out of.'

A many-versed Catholic hymn is sung, and the younger boys struggle to work out which page they are on. The Mass begins, and the boys in the Schola Cantorum, red and white in their cassocks and cottas, sing the Gloria.

How can I get my boy into the Schola? think the mothers. Maybe get him singing lessons, or send him on a course somewhere. I must e-mail Mr Cole and ask him how the audition system works.

'Sit down.'

That's the voice of the headmaster. The boys instantly sit down, and the parents, too, are happy to obey the order. He's one of the leading prep-school headmasters in London. And just think, he was a boy here once! The boys seem to revere him. He's got that innate gift of authority, doesn't need to shout at them.

Father Dominic gives a homily. He asks the boys to put their hands up, and they dredge their religious knowledge to come up with the right answer.

'Faith.'

'Nearly, but not quite. Yes, Patrick?'

'Grace.'

'That's right. Grace.'

Adorable. It's good for boys to know these things. There's moral backbone at this place. The boys learn to love going to Mass. It helps that it's instead of lessons. And, as Father Dominic says, 'Even if they reject religion in their teens, they'll know exactly what they're rejecting.'

The boys must be getting hungry for their packed lunches. No chocolate or fizzy drinks allowed. No-nut policy, of course. Mine's got a ham roll today, and a flapjack.

'Kneel down.'

The prayers of the Mass begin. Everyone prays fervently. Every parent knows someone who's suffering from cancer. Terrifying. The Royal Marsden is down the road. There but for the Grace of God go we. The boys from the Schola come down and kneel before the altar. The few Anglican boys get a pat on the head and

a blessing. The choirboys go back up to the gallery and sing some ethereal Palestrina, and it's the turn of the blue-blazered boys to line up on their knees in front of the altar. Then it's the parents' turn, and the Anglican mothers (I am one) sit tight in the pews, wishing the two churches weren't divided. So near yet so far. The Pope and the Archbishop of Canterbury actually embraced each other in Westminster Abbey recently.

As the organ voluntary plays at the end, the headmaster (purely by gesture) orchestrates the boys into a symmetrical two-at-a-time genuflection and exit. It's the best spectacle in town. Everyone feels a sense of post-eucharistic elation.

Mr Tibbits (buried in Warwick) would definitely approve.

Afterword

To be a child in post-war London was to live in a strange and haunted place, particularly as the ghosts were difficult to define. I had been born in Cairo in 1949, when my father was working in the Embassy there, and I arrived in Wetherby Place as a baby in 1951. We lived in a tall, red-brick house, the last in the row, just at the point where the street connected with the stuccoed and more prosperous-looking houses of Hereford Square. Later, this would be rather a smart address but in the early '50s more or less nowhere was smart. If anyone can believe it, behind the houses on the west side of the square was a field where I seem to remember someone kept a pony. And on the edge of that field was a cottage, left over from a stabling arrangement of a hundred years before, where, in my time, an actor lived with his potter wife. I do not remember that the actor ever worked much, but they were nice people and she used to allow us to model things with her clay which would then be baked, painted (by us) and glazed (by her), to serve as an unending supply of rather ugly and squashed presents for my patient Mama.

In that era, there was a sense about London of the morning after the night before, a feeling that the citizens were still checking to see that their heads remained on their shoulders. Once elegant thoroughfares and terraces had gaps in their smiles, which were sometimes, but not always, boarded off from trespass, though no one took these warnings very seriously. The corner of Hereford Square opposite our front door was a vast crater, with a few battered stubs of walls around the edge, and there were similar sights in Harrington Gardens, to the back of us, and along the Old Brompton Road. These bombsites were slightly bewildering to us children, as we had missed the conflict that caused them. They seemed simply part of the city we grew up in, like the detritus of a Battle of the Giants from some long ago time, but it was clear that they represented a very real and still vivid episode to our parents, whose faith had been severely shaken by the tumultuous events they represented.

But strangely perhaps, and after months of shaking off the dust and making sure it was once again safe to go outside, people started tentatively to live their real lives again. And in those early years, there came about a misleading impression that, somehow, miraculously to the fortunate few, it seemed that the old life had survived. Some families threw in the towel and country houses began to flood the market, but others cleaned up and swept up and returned to a version of their former existence, their resolve gathering pace with every year that passed. White tie, banished from wartime ballrooms in favour of the uniform, made its reappearance in the summer of 1950 and gathered pace thereafter, and I can remember my parents coming into the nursery on the way to some *grande galère*, he in tails, she in a new evening dress of pale blue silk, with pearl-embroidered straps, in about 1952 or '53, asking for our infantile approval and obviously delighted by a sense of The Return of Things Properly Done, although I would not then have understood their joy.

To reassure them further, the revival of Presentation meant that the débutante Season, aslumber through the war years, seemed once again to have a future – albeit a slightly muted one, with garden parties replacing the evening courts – and friends of my mother who had no London end would arrive with suitcases and hat boxes and shut themselves and their daughters into our spare room to change. I can still remember standing as a small boy watching those beautiful young girls coming downstairs, their wide, New Look skirts bouncing gently on layered petticoats around their stockinged legs, their wide hats shading carefully made-up faces, with smooth, powdered complexions and bright red lips.

It was of course a chimera. For those who hankered after a return to the pre-war world, the decade of the 1950s was a false dawn. The very basic changes that the war had made, or had begun to make, in people's expectations would only manifest themselves as things eased up, socially and financially, in the 1960s, but they were already germinating from the day peace was declared. I can only say it did not seem so then. At least not to a child. And in this strange mixed atmosphere of deceived relief, the schools came back to the city and gradually reopened, bringing, I think now at this distance, another sense of returning calm to our parents. The boys and girls wore the neat uniforms from before the war and much the same lessons were taught as were taught in the late 1930s, making them feel that perhaps civilization had not after all been destroyed, but instead only put to sleep for a while. Russell's, or Wetherby School as it was more formally known, set up across the road from us, with the rather nice and chubby Mrs Russell in charge, aided and abetted by her considerably less nice and cadaverous husband, a figure of fear in the neighbourhood. Then, when we had finished our nursery teachings, Mr Tibbits's school, four doors down, on the same pavement as our house, claimed us Fellowes boys, one after another.

Mr Tibbits was well suited to the 1950s notion that the world had not changed much. He was a stern figure to me and I read with some surprise that other boys thought him friendly. He had that fervour about his faith that seems to be reserved for Saints suffering persecution, or for converts, and had little in common with my parents' more moderate belief in an essentially reasonable God.

The school already had a strong affiliation with the Brompton Oratory which to this day means that when I enter that vast edifice I feel like a small boy, simultaneously overwhelmed and bored by its magnificence. Mrs Tibbits was also a severe figure and not one of those headmistresses who offset their husband's strictures by an exaggerated tenderness towards the children in their care. But they were not cruel, or not that I remember. Even when my brothers and I were beaten for being consistently late in the mornings, I cannot pretend we resented it much, since we had for some time been what would now be termed 'pushing our luck'. Above all, they believed in order, in rules and manners and traditions, and having lived into the Age of Disorder, I sympathize with them today a little more than I did then.

But if the Tibbits pair presented a sober and even opaque face to the world, there were elements to our life at the school that were less than orthodox. We used to play games on some far-flung field (might it have been in Wimbledon?) and one of the residents whose garden abutted it, used to throw old *Health and Efficiency* magazines over the fence to lie there, in a tempting pile, for us pre-pubescent tots to sneak a look at. The trick was to run round after the ball, stretching the circuit to allow a view of those nice, pretty girls throwing their beach balls in air-brushed innocence. I seem to recall we got quite good at doing this without attracting the attention of the games master. And the teaching staff boasted some unusual personalities, not to say eccentrics, who stand out in my memory. We quite liked the rather dour Mr Atkinson who seemed then, and I suspect now, to be having too little fun. And we loved one teacher in particular who received, via a telegram delivered to him in class, the news of his father's death and consequent inheritance. With a cry of 'Yippee!' he flung the cable into the air, jumped up, left the room and was never seen again.

I have told earlier how my love of history was born during my Tibbits years, and I made good friends, too.

One, Adam Bowen, now a television and film-maker in Sydney, remains a friend to this day. But, in the end, my abiding sense of the Tibbits's time was one of an ordered world. We did what we were told, we wore what we were told, and I suspect we gave a false impression to our parents that it would always be so – that we would be as obedient to their commands and wishes as they had been to our grandparents' generation in the late Teens and Twenties when they were growing up. It was not to be. In March 1963, John Profumo would declare in the House of Commons that there was 'no impropriety whatever' in his relationship with Christine Keeler. The resulting scandal would blow the aristocratic establishment out of government and, by a supreme irony, that same month saw the release of the Beatles' first album, *Please Please Me*, heralding the youth revolution all set to engulf the whole of Europe and America and to bury the Old World forever. St Philip's would survive, and lives on now, but the values that sustained it half a century ago, the confident and sedate landscape of my childhood, for good or ill, are as dead as the Dodo.

JULIAN FELLOWES

Acknowledgements

I am immensely grateful to every person quoted in the book, each of whom spared time to talk to me and gave me invaluable insights. Special thanks to: Harry and Anna Biggs-Davison, Denise Bolam, Christopher Gardner-Thorpe, Clare Hill, Louis Jebb, Father Rupert McHardy, Michael Maxtone-Smith, Robert and Claudia Maxtone Graham, John Milward, Harriet Mould, Harriot Rennie and Roger Taylor. Deepest thanks also to Gail Pirkis, Hazel Wood and all the staff at *Slightly Foxed*.

About the Author

Ysenda Maxtone Graham is an author and journalist, who has written widely for the *Sunday Telegraph*, the *Sunday Express* and the *Evening Standard*, among many other publications. She is the author of *The Church Hesitant: A Portrait of the Church of England Today*, and of *The Real Mrs Miniver*, a biography of her grandmother Jan Struther, which was shortlisted for the Whitbread Biography of the Year in 2002. She lives in London with her husband and their three sons.

SLIGHTLY FOXED EDITIONS

Slightly Foxed Editions are published by
Slightly Foxed Limited.
For more information please contact us at:

67 Dickinson Court
15 Brewhouse Yard
London ECIV 4JX

tel 020 7549 2121/2111
fax 0870 1991245
e-mail all@foxedquarterly.com
www.foxedquarterly.com